OVERCOMING

OVERCOMING
STORIES OF TRIUMPH THROUGH FAITH

LINDA STEPHENS-JONES

Published by Richard 'Spike' Jones
Raleigh, North Carolina

Scripture quotations, unless noted otherwise, are taken from the Holy Bible: New International Version. Copyright © 1973, 1978, 1987, International Bible Society.

Overcoming: Stories of Triumph Through Faith/Linda Stephens-Jones, First Edition

978-0-9992505-2-5 (Paperback)
978-0-9992505-3-2 (eBook)

This book is dedicated to each of the inspiring overcomers, who were a part of this project, the persons who shared their challenges and stories of overcoming so openly in the spirit of encouraging and giving hope to others.

To those who shared their story and have now gone home to Glory, I'm so thankful that you entrusted me with your story. It can now fall into the hands of someone who needs the hope and encouragement that you lived as an overcomer.

CONTENTS

Foreword...xi

Introduction xv

CHAPTER ONE: OVERCOMING IN RELATIONSHIPS 1

A Lifetime Together – *Jim and Jean Jones*...................2

A Legacy of Faith – *Rochella Marable* 10

Seasons of Marriage – *Rev. Jeffery & Brenda Gaines*.............17

Your Mindset Matters – *Joseph 'Joe' Alexander*.......................27

Leaping Over Limiting Beliefs – *Rev. Alan Harris*.................33

CHAPTER TWO: OVERCOMING IN CAREER MATTERS 41

Gifted to Serve Through Music – *Curtis Taylor Sr.* 42

The Key to Finding Contentment – *Dale Fletcher* 50

One Door Closes. Another Door Opens – *Keitha Johnson*....57

Reaching Your True Potential – *Anthony 'Tony' Stamilio*......64

From Challenges to Blessings – *Rev. Dr. Marshal Ausberry*..70

Dwell in Possibility – *Toni Townes-Whitley*.............................78

CHAPTER THREE: OVERCOMING HEALTH CHALLENGES 87

Seeing Challenges as Preparation – *Dr. Joe Lee* 88

Life Changing Health Challenges – *Mark and Brenda Moore* 96

Caring for Your Mind Body and Spirit – *Felicea Myer-DeLoatch* 105

Living in the Midst of a Miracle – *Mel and Cecelia Mann* .. 113

A Formula for Peace – *Linda Eatmon-Jones* 122

Trusting God Despite the Odds – *Janice LaVore-Fletcher* ... 129

CHAPTER FOUR: OVERCOMING UNCERTAINTY AND RISK 137

The Power of Forgiveness – *Alia Watkins* 138

Triumph Over Obstacles – *Rev. Michael Coppedge* 146

A Matter of Choices – *Lonnie Williams* 154

A Spirit of Resilience – *Rev. Lou Phillips* 161

Be the Change You Want to See: Part I – *Joanne Latimer* ... 169

CHAPTER FIVE: OVERCOMING WHILE SERVING 177

How Do You Multiply? – *Tony Small* 178

Destined to Serve God's People – *Deacon Lawrence 'Larry' Hester* 186

Be the Change You Want to See: Part II – *Jameece Pinckney* 194

Fulfillment Awaits – *Rev. Cozy Bailey* 203

What Story Do You Want Your Life to Tell? – *Michael Marx* 211

BONUS: WISDOM OF A 93-YEAR OLD..**219**

Faith Manifested Over a Lifetime – *Mrs. Pennia*
　　'Penny Bell' Ford...220

More on the Overcomers..233

Acknowledgments...237

FOREWORD

I am Rev Jim Harden, and I am Associate Minister at the Antioch Baptist Church (ABC) in Fairfax Station, VA, where I also serve as the Dean and Founding Co-Director of the Antioch Bible Institute (ABI), a three-year intensive study of the Old Testament, New Testament, and Theology. I have a BS in Management and Leadership from Wayland Baptist University; a MA in Business Administration from Webster University; and a MDiv from the Samuel Dewitt Proctor School of Theology at Virginia Union University. I am a Hospital Chaplain, having completed my internship in Clinical Pastoral Education (CPE) at the National Institutes of Health and my CPE Residency at Georgetown University Hospital. I have known and served with Linda and her husband, Richard 'Spike' Jones, since they joined Antioch in 1999.

Linda and Spike soon became regular attendees and eventually members of ABC. At the time, they were both senior civilian government employees, Linda with the U.S. Air Force and Spike with the U.S. Army. They began serving in various ministries and were eventually selected as Deacon and Deaconess at our church, providing spiritual care and support for a specified group of our members, including my wife and me. They were enthusiastic, compassionate, and empathetic leaders. Our relationship has grown over the years from a mere partnership in ministry to true friendship. I watched their Christian growth as their walk with God and their marriage have matured. I witnessed their transformation from new members to involved, caring, and engaged Christian Community Leaders far beyond the walls of the church.

In 2008 they joined the Antioch Bible Institute to gain a deeper and more comprehensive knowledge of Christ and how to apply the bible in their daily lives. They were loyal and attentive students always eager to learn more about service to Almighty God. During this same period, Linda and Spike had become full-time caregivers for Linda's mother, and we often prayed and counseled together. Even amidst the pain of her mother's decline due to dementia, Linda was always ready, willing, and fully able to share insightful and caring advice where needed.

A year after their graduation from ABI in June 2011, Linda retired from her federal career to have more time with her mother. Her Christian ethic, leadership background and her passions for both the Word of God and His people ignited her interest in a second career where she could openly integrate and share her faith. As Linda saw others struggling with a season of caregiving, nearing retirement, relationships with adult children or other mid-life issues, Linda began to seek my advice about pursuing a new career path as a Christian Life Coach. I felt that her impressive history, empathy, and love for others made her perfect for this type of work. I was confident that she was a natural. She didn't stop there and has since pursued training to become credentialed as an ICF Professional Certified Coach. She is a speaker & trainer, while still also offering faith-based coaching.

When Linda's mother transitioned to Glory, we shared time in conference with each other as I helped her journey through her loss and pain of that period. Over the following years, especially since completing her training and certification, I have watched her grow exponentially through her work coaching with a myriad of clients and conducting the deeply personal interviews that are the genesis of this book. She has blossomed as an established, caring, professional coach, wife, servant leader, and woman of God. I have profoundly appreciated her contributions to her ministry, family, friends, community, church, and others.

Many of the stories in this book are about people I know very well, and I have an ongoing personal Christian relationship with several. Linda's obedience to the nudges of the Holy Spirit to create narratives from the earlier interviews, will allow readers to take a uniquely helpful and insightful journey through the lives of Godly individuals whose experiences have provided them with such useful, life altering, and meaningful lessons such as The Power of Forgiveness, How to Gain Fulfillment, Finding Contentment, and Serving God's People.

I firmly believe that the lessons of our lives can be learned in different ways. We can actually live various experiences for ourselves, which can be painful. Alternatively, we can hear and/

or read about the experiences of others and benefit from what they have learned as they went through the same or similar experiences, which to me is far less difficult and painful. In these pages are the thoughts, actions, behaviors, and ultimate experiences of some people who have been through or may be going through something similar to what you are (or may soon be) experiencing! Read here and learn some insights about their OVERCOMING!!!!

Rev. Jim Harden

INTRODUCTION

Have you ever had a nudge in your spirit that you're supposed to do something, but you don't feel fully capable of doing it? That was me about writing this book. I had a second career that I loved as a Christian Life Coach. In addition to coaching, had the opportunity to interview numerous people about their lives over a couple of years in a podcast.

A couple of years after I stopped doing the interviews, the nudge began. I sensed that what had been shared with me in those interviews could be put into a book as stories of triumph through faith that could be read and shared over and over again! And not only shared, but they could encourage and uplift people who felt alone, or who felt dismal about their life situations. When we are going through tough times in life, we can feel that we're the only one, or that no one else would understand. But I knew that we have all had or are having tough trials in our lives. I believed it was worth it to try, and thankfully many of the people I interviewed gave their permission to have some of what they shared with me, repurposed into story form, for the book that you are holding now. Through these stories, you will see their trials, feel their pain, and be uplifted by how they overcame very difficult challenges.

The problem was I was not a writer. But as a coach, I help people to overcome self-doubt, and to take steps to put their faith into action, how to get out of their comfort zones to pursue purpose, achieve their goals and feel more of the fulfillment that they desire in their lives. So, I had to practice what I coached! While speaking at the Women's Ministry Christmas Program at my church in December 2018, I made a declaration that I would be writing this book! I said it believing that God had been nudging me to do this and that although I wasn't a writer, He would equip me. Once I made that public declaration, I prayed and trusted it was not too big for God to help me to bring the vision of this book of uplifting stories to reality. I remembered what God has done in my life before. Writing was out of my comfort zone, but God gave me this assignment and I can truly say, He equipped me!! I hope my testimony speaks to someone who is being nudged about something who is afraid to get out of their comfort zones.

These stories are not full biographies, but snapshots that let readers step inside the lives of these individuals, to learn some of their background and perspectives as they dealt with some specific challenges, and especially to see the role that faith played in overcoming their stressful situations. At the end of each story, there are a few questions that will let readers to reflect upon their own journeys and find meaningful personal application.

There is a bonus story of a beloved 93-year-old woman of great wisdom, love, inspiration and faith at the end of the book that I don't want you to miss. May you feel the depth of her wisdom and let hers and all the stories speak to you! And if you know someone who needs encouragement, I hope you'll share these stories with them.

In this current season in your life, no matter how dark or difficult right now, I believe you can still have hope, you can still heal, forgive, renew yourself, find purpose and peace through a relationship with and faith in Jesus Christ.

With Love & Blessings,

Linda

CHAPTER ONE

OVERCOMING IN RELATIONSHIPS

My beloved is mine and I am his; he browses among the lilies.
(Song of Songs 2:16)

Picture this. A seven-year-old girl was walking over to her grandfather's house, and by the pond in front of his house, she saw this young boy sitting and throwing stones into the water, watching the ripples. Being the confident child that she was, before going into her grandfather's house, she walked out to the pond, straight up to the boy and introduced herself.

Jean saw a maturity in this boy, who turned out to be nine years old. She had seen this boy a couple of days earlier when she was hanging clothes on the line with her mother at their home in Marion Station, Maryland. She saw a mule drawing a cart with children and a mother and father walking behind the cart coming into their neighborhood. She asked her mother who they were, and was told that they were the new Jones family, moving into an abandoned schoolhouse.

At the pond they talked for about a minute, and the young boy looked at the confident little girl and told her, "You know, I want to move away from here one day and I want to make something of myself." The little girl replied, "Well that's good." And so, it began…the shared life path of Jim and Jean Jones which is still going strong after 54 years of marriage, three children and seven grandchildren. (24 years to 15 months).

Jean's family had a bit more in the way of resources than Jim's family did. Her Mom was the church pianist, and both of her parents were focused on Jean being the first in her family to attend college. They had a car and a party-line phone. Jim knew his family was poor. They were not able to settle down in one home as the poor conditions of a house frequently caused them to have to move again and again. Jim equated his family and groups of other families like his, as similar to today's migrant workers who also moved wherever they could find work. His tough growing up years motivated him to work hard, determined to get out of that kind of harsh and unpredictable environment.

Jim and Jean went from elementary school on through high school together. They both took the school bus and that was their time to talk and get to know each other. Jim thought Jean was cute and very smart, and Jean thought Jim was smart and a great athlete. They were really good friends, as that was the extent to which Jean's parents would allow. Jim and Jean did get away with holding hands in the back of her grandfather's old Model T car on their way to church. Because Jim's parents had few means for Jim and his four siblings, Jean was concerned he didn't get enough to eat. She recalled making peanut butter and jelly or bologna sandwiches and hiding the sandwiches inside her blouse to sneak them out of the house to take to him, and Jim decided to 'hook his wagon to hers' because he knew she was going somewhere!

From early on, this couple had grown up with and continued to embrace certain core values. For Jean, God and the church had always been present in her life, (her Mom faithfully served as the church pianist for over 60 years), and the family consistently prayed and studied the bible. For Jim, when his family moved to Jean's town when he was nine, the songs and prayers in church as well as the school devotions before classes appealed to him and set the tone for the day.

Both valued the love of their parents, a closely connected community, and caring teachers (in segregated schools) who contributed to their developing high standards of excellence and becoming good citizens. To this day, Jim and Jean value having God as the center in their lives, along with their unconditional love, open communication, lots of trust and lots of prayer.

After high school, they both attended Morgan State University, with Jim beginning there a couple of years before Jean. During his last year, Jim was hit with a challenge that shifted the course of his future. The registrar's office inadvertently billed him for a tuition balance that actually belonged to someone else, and he had to leave college before he graduated. Jean got personally involved in reviewing the records until the billing error was found and rectified. But by that point, Jim had already left college and enlisted in the Army.

This was the one period where it seemed that Jim and Jean's lives might go in separate directions. Jim even began dating and got engaged to another young lady. But during Jean's senior year, Jim showed up (in uniform) on campus and professed to Jean that she was the one he had always loved. Smartly, Jim broke off the other engagement and asked Jean to marry him.

Jim went on to do a full military career of 33 years, retiring at the rank of Colonel (0-6). While in the Army, he had the opportunity to go back to finish his undergraduate and graduate degrees at Morgan State University. Jim and Jean also received Honorary Doctorate degrees from Morgan State in 2015 for their pioneering, courageous work during the Civil Rights Movement. They both spent 3 days in jail while at Morgan State College for their participation in sit - ins and picketing in 1963.

Jim and Jean's love and 'like' for one another have cemented their bond. But further, their shared interests as well as their faith have carried them through every season and chapter of their lives, including the valleys. And they have had a few.

Jean shared one difficult valley season which occurred while they were still newlyweds in March of 1967, when within four months of their marriage, Jim had to go to Vietnam. He arrived in Vietnam during the period of the Tet Offensive, when hundreds of soldiers were being killed every week. Her heart sank when Jim told her the news. After Jim was in Vietnam, she received a dreaded call in the middle of a Friday night from the Red Cross, that Jim had been wounded. She fell to her knees because she knew the power of prayer, so that was her first response. She prayed all weekend and had family and others praying with her. The next call did not come until Monday, when the Red Cross called back to say that he had been shot in the arm but that he was okay. Their next words made her angry, but they made her laugh at the same time. They told her that Jim refused to leave his troops. He refused to be evacuated. Jean smiled and knew that was "her Jim."

Between his two tours in Vietnam, Jim came home for a year and Jean was pregnant when he left again. Jean remembered times when she'd call her mom with her fear and uncertainty of Jim being in a war zone and her pregnant. Jean would ask her mom, "What am I going to do?" Her mom's reply was always the same; a pause and then the question, "Where is your faith?" This made Jean continue to deepen and depend upon faith through every challenge.

When Jim returned from his second year-long tour in Vietnam in November of 1971, things were very challenging at home. Jean saw a different Jim who was anxious, nervous and he drove his car much too fast. He even frightened her during an argument once with a very intense tone of voice. They eventually recognized the need to pull together as a family through the challenges of having been separated for such a period and the significant aftereffects of Jim having served in combat. Jim had experienced living in the day-to-day combat setting and as an infantry officer, he became accustomed to the constant threats of a war zone. But he later came to understand the toll on his family and countless other families hearing recurring reports of hundreds being killed in a week's time.

The Joneses saw challenges much like any other family during the seasons of raising three children. But today, they see the blessings of their children who live near them, whom they describe as wonderful, college educated adults with successful careers and beautiful kids of their own now.

Another substantial challenge the Joneses faced together was one of health, as they both received cancer diagnoses within a three-week time period. Jim was diagnosed with prostate cancer and Jean with breast cancer. When Jean told Jim her diagnosis, he made her laugh with, "Listen, I can't have any-thing without you having it too." They shared a laugh and did what they always did: they were there for each other and stood together. Jim had surgery on October 2nd and Jean had surgery three weeks later on Oct 22nd. Both still had demanding jobs during their rounds of treatment. It was a very difficult time, but they took care of each other. They reminisced on the way that when either of them was down, the other was there to uplift and provide loving support.

During their journeys with cancer, they took the time to sit together, read the bible and pray together. They surrounded themselves with their loving children, other family, church family and close friends. Jim and Jean survived their bouts with cancer and have been cancer survivors for 12 years. Ultimately, the Joneses saw their battles with cancer as a time when God brought them even closer together. And they demonstrated their faith and continued to encourage and uplift others as they went through their own battles. Praise the Lord!

Today, the Joneses continue to maintain busy schedules, committed to sharing their love, wisdom and service to others. Their lifestyle shows a model of loving one another and loving God. Through every phase of life, every blessing, every chal-lenge, and choice in life, Jim and Jean Jones cling to their faith in God and to each other.

Because of their loving marriage of over 54 years at the time of our conversation, who better to share a *Top 10 Ways to Have a Happy Marriage* than Jim and Jean? Some of the list has been mentioned in this story, but here are the 'Happy Marriage Cliffs Notes,' courtesy of the Joneses:

1. Share a faith in God
2. Learn to pray together.
3. Share unconditional love.
4. Find common interests. Don't spend lots of your time on separate interests. Learn to enjoy things your spouse enjoys so that you can enjoy them together. 'Like' one another.
5. Support each other through the good days and the difficult days.
6. Make intimacy with each other a priority.
7. Do not speak badly about each other in front of others. "No airing your dirty laundry." Express your concerns or disagreements in private.
8. Do not keep secrets from each other. Have open communication.
9. Have date nights. And weekends away. Carve out your getaway times to spend together.
10. Have lots of trust in each other.

REFLECTIONS FOR YOU:

1. What do you want to apply to your life from Jim & Jean's story?

2. What impact could it have on your marriage if you two came together to pray?

3. What is an interest that you & your spouse both have that you could enjoy together?

A LEGACY OF FAITH – ROCHELLA MARABLE

As each has received a gift, use it to serve one another, as good stewards of God's varied grace: whoever speaks, as one who speaks oracles of God; whoever serves, as one who serves by the strength that God supplies—in order that in everything God may be glorified through Jesus Christ. To him belong glory and dominion forever and ever. (Peter 4:10-11)

When a Christian sister was asked to share her core values, what she shared was truly inspiring! It was inspiring because of her clarity and because it's what we see her live. She responded this way: "My core value is to love the Lord with all my heart, with all my soul and with all my mind; to serve Him with a grateful heart, to bring glory to God in everything I do, for Him and serving Him, serving my family, my children, my grandchildren and the Kingdom family."

Rochella Marable is that Christian sister. This is her story, derived from a conversation right after Mother's Day some years ago. We looked back at her childhood, and the lessons and legacy of her mother. We discussed her faith, her own mothering, and her current blessed season as a grandmother and the legacy she desires to leave.

Rochella Marable is a Georgia peach, who grew up in the Booker T. Washington housing in Columbus, GA and there she completed high school. Her dad, incredibly hard-working, was a warehouse man for the local government. Her mom was a housewife who also worked outside their home as a maid.

Her parents were Christians and they served faithfully at St Mark A.M.E. Church. Rochella and her siblings participated in all of the church's activities, and she was a leader as they grew up in the church. Her mother always had dinner ready, and the kids could not eat until their father got home. Her mother was a wonderful housekeeper, wife and mother. Both of Rochella's parents believed in Christ and read the Word of God. Their family had a strong foundation based on faith and loving Christ.

Rochella was a very determined, strong willed and committed girl with dreams of being a teacher or social worker. Although not many colleges were integrated, her desire was to attend William and Mary College because of their premier social work program. Little did Rochella know at the time the plans that the Lord had in store for her.

Rochella described her mother as a fearless, godly woman, who believed in the power of prayer and trusted the Lord with all her heart. Even though they lived in the Jim Crow South, her mother was courageous and did not fear anyone regardless of their race. Her mother was the disciplinarian in the family, yet her heart was always compassionate toward others who had less. She often shared from whatever they had, which was not that much, to give to neighbors who had nothing. And she gave without expecting anything in return.

Unfortunately, Rochella's mother grew up without knowing her own mother. So, Mother's Day was a sad time for her. Even as a child, Rochella did everything she could to make Mother's Day a special day for her mother. She vividly recalled one year while still in elementary school; she entered a radio contest by writing a letter about her Mother. Her entry won and her Mother was showered with flowers and gifts from high end stores in downtown Columbus, Georgia!!

Rochella and her husband Renard, have been blessed with three children. She wanted to instill a foundation in her children to have respect, integrity (to let their word be their bond) and trust in God; to stand on His promises and to be an example in society. Her children and their spouses are enjoying success in their lives and chosen careers. Rochella and Renard laid a foundation that everything they received was not about what they did, but what God was able to do in their lives. She always wanted her children to embrace Proverbs 3:5-6, *Trust in the Lord with all your heart, and do not lean on your own understanding. In all your ways acknowledge him, and he will make straight your paths.* Rochella knew her children would note that she was also a strong disciplinarian when they were growing up...the influence of her mother.

Today, Rochella relishes her role as a grandmother of six sweet grandchildren whom she calls her sugar babies. Kennedy, Chase, Miles, Ella, William Renard, and Bronwyn, at the time of our discussion were aged from eleven down to a one-year-old. Her children taught her many lessons that she now passes on to her grandchildren. Rochella has devotion with her grandbabies and when they greet each other daily, it is done this way, "This is the day that the Lord has made. We shall rejoice and be glad in it." Rochella pours the seeds of faith into her sugar babies in a very hands-on manner. She told her children about

God's Word, but with her grandchildren, she shows them. She buys each of them a Bible when they reach kindergarten age. Rochella sits with them, and she teaches them about God's Word, instilling in them that God's Word will always be with them.

Rochella's faith and trust in Christ have been tested and proven as she has walked through difficult valley moments in her life, a few of which she discussed. Her toughest trials have been the loss of her father, mother and sister. And she almost lost her husband, the love of her life in 2014.

When the doctor told Rochella's beloved and only sister that they had done all they could do for her illness, Rochella was with her at the hospital. She took care of her sister until she passed away a short time later and remained in Georgia through her sister's funeral rites. It was very hard for Rochella because when she retired from her federal government career in July 2009, she thought she and her sister would have a lot of wonderful times together, but little did they know, her sister only had months to live. She passed away in October 2009. Afterwards, Rochella made it a point to continue to pour into her sister's children. They are doing well, having a foundation of believing and trusting in God, just as Rochella's mother had planted into Rochella and all of her siblings.

Because of the prognosis of her sister, Rochella had to leave the planning for an upcoming women's conference at her home church to her ministry team. She returned to Virginia in time to open the women's conference. She knew it was only through prayer and faith that she experienced what she did when she got back to Virginia. Even though she had lost her only sister, when she walked into the church, she immediately felt like she had a church full of sisters who blessed her!

Then in 2014, the plight of almost losing her husband occurred. Rochella and her husband had been through a lot of seasons filled with trouble, many battles, and a lot of empty moments in their relationship. But when her husband became ill, they were in a season of roses, and kisses and joy. Rochella's husband went into the hospital for surgery, and as she prepared to go home once the surgery was over and deemed successful, she said she would be back the next day to bring him home. Instead, she later got a phone call that they had rushed her husband to intensive care, and it was a touch-and-go situation. Rochella was completely caught off guard and she totally relied on her faith and trust in the Lord. She prayed and sent out a prayer request for others to pray for her husband. Through God's grace, over a period of two months her husband fully recovered!

On a personal observation, I watched first-hand as Rochella showed the depth of her faith during another challenging period. She was going through some health examinations herself and her condition was potentially kidney cancer. I went over to her after church to encourage her and to let her know that I would be praying for her. Her response was unforgettable. She was very calm and said that she prayed for God's will to be fulfilled. And she said that all I needed to do for her was to pray for God's will to be fulfilled. What an impact that had on my faith, that as Rochella faced a potentially life-threatening situation of her own, she was calm, confident and secure in her faith.

Rochella demonstrated her faith even in the midst of these unforeseen circumstances, when her plans with her sister and husband did not go as she expected. But how? It was not easy, but Rochella learned from her mother to never give up. Just like her mother, she stood on her faith and was determined. She attributed her determination and faith as "the apple doesn't fall far from the tree," - a part of her legacy of faith.

Although Rochella did not get to pursue a degree at William & Mary College, as a military spouse she got to live in different parts of the world and successfully complete a 23-year federal career in 2009. Today she is a joyful servant of the Lord, with a Master of Business Administration (MBA) from Lincoln University and a Master's in Theological Studies from Liberty University. Rochella is a passionate Bible study teacher. She shares God's good news in her church community, with women in a county detention center, as well as abroad on mission trips to Kenya, Senegal, Brazil and Antigua. Additionally, Rochella has furthered her biblical knowledge as a diligent student with travel to the Holy Land, Greece, Egypt and Turkey.

So, what did we observe when we looked inside the life of a Christian woman who lived the roles of daughter, sister, wife, mother, grandmother and servant of God? We saw a girl raised by Christian parents, who was involved in church activities as she grew up, and who saw examples of living faith and trust in the Lord above all else. A woman who got married and instilled Christian virtues and beliefs in her children when she became a mother, A woman who cherishes her roles as servant of God and loving grandmother who is directly teaching her grandchildren about Christ. Further, we see a woman who has a thirst for knowledge of and a growing relationship with Christ. She is one who has demonstrated her faith in service to others near and far, and in the midst of the trials and challenges of life. Through Rochella Marable, we witness a legacy of faith!

REFLECTIONS FOR YOU:

1. What does Rochella's story cause you to reminisce about in your life?

2. What are the key values and lessons that you desire to pass down to your children and grandchildren?

3. When you think of your legacy (what you leave behind), what do you want it to be?

SEASONS OF MARRIAGE - REV. JEFFERY & BRENDA GAINES

For everything there is a season, a time for every activity under heaven. A time to weep and a time to laugh. A time to mourn and a time to dance. A time to tear and a time to mend. A time to be quiet and a time to speak. (Ecclesiastes 3:1, 4 & 7)

Marriage has distinct seasons almost akin to the four seasons in a calendar year, although the seasons of marriage may not present with the predictability of the weather. Married couples commonly experience adjustments early in their marriage as they get to know each other, but as they have children, their focus and communication styles may change and this equally applies with a myriad of seasons such as health challenges, career development, adult children, grandchildren, grief and loss, empty nesting, relocations and retirement. Each season comes with its own blessings and challenges, but for a marriage to thrive in the long run, it takes cultivating the habits of having faith in God and serving and supporting each other.

Rev. Jeffery and Brenda Gaines shared relatable examples of some of their seasons over 31-plus years of marriage. Jeff and Brenda met for the first time as a five and a six-year-old. They have known each other for over 50 years. That turned into a blessing as they were fortunate to grow up together. The couple embodies a deep faith, love for the Lord and family and service to others.

Brenda is a veteran and retired federal employee whose career culminated as a senior adviser to the U.S. Army Surgeon

General and other Army senior Health Affairs executives. She is now the CEO of her own company, BG Consulting Services LLC. At the time of our interview, Jeff, an Army retiree (military intelligence specialty), worked as a federal intelligence educator in the Office of the Director of National Intelligence. He was also enrolled in seminary, working on a Master's Degree in Practical Theology. Jeff was called into ministry in 1990 and became an ordained minister in 1998.

With loads of career achievements, Jeff and Brenda were living with joy and contentment in their present season with two adult children, a daughter-in-law, a grandson and new grandbaby on the way. Both Jeff and Brenda emphasized this was a season of abundant blessings in their lives, where they sought ways that they could give to others, how they could serve and be a blessing to others.

So far it sounded like this couple had almost magically arrived at this blessed season in their lives. But such was not the case. Jeff and Brenda openly shared examples of times of trials and how they have overcome difficult seasons through their years together.

Brenda first described a recent season of difficulty. At a time when she loved her career, where she led the establishment and operational management of thirteen intricate executive agencies, she made the decision to retire, to be able to spend more time with her father who had been diagnosed with an aggressive form of cancer. Just three weeks after retiring from her federal career, Brenda's father died suddenly. She had lost her mother a few years earlier, but her father had continued to hold their family together.

Within a matter of weeks, Brenda felt she had lost her sense of identity, not only due to the end of her career, but due to the sudden loss of her father. She described feeling like an orphan. The very confident self-assured woman now felt lost, struggling to find new air, without her powerful job and the presence of her father and mother. Brenda's father had also been like a father to Jeff, so he too was grieving his own personal loss. Fortunately, they were able to navigate through her Dad's illness and his passing together. They had made individual trips to visit Brenda's Dad earlier, while the other kept things going in their home for their children who also had known and loved their grandfather.

At this key crossroads, Brenda opted to hire a Christian life coach whom she worked with for six months. She described it as a most pivotal point which helped her to refocus on who she still remained as wife, mother, grandmother and business owner. Brenda began to reach out to God in a stronger manner than ever. She not only found her identity again, but she found herself in God in a much stronger way. The other factor that really helped Brenda during this dark time was that she leaned into her husband, her family and close circle of friends, her prayer partner and pastor. She knitted herself around those who loved and cared about her. In what had been a most difficult and bleak time, out of it, Brenda morphed into a butterfly again!

Jeff's personal example of living through tough times was his childhood. His early years were not a pleasant environment, and he ended up failing school and ultimately dropping out. From there Jeff joined the military, a transitional moment for him, because his military leadership told him to go back to school. Jeff went back to school but struggled because of his low reading skills and lack of confidence. Certain teachers even told him he would not succeed in life. Further, without a positive model of what a good husband and father looked like, Jeff came into their marriage with some of the baggage from his early years. He at times mimicked the (bad) examples he had seen. And sometimes even his attempts to model a different role as a husband did not all land well either. Jeff had to learn a lot of lessons in his role as husband. Brenda had grown up in a stable and loving, middle-class home with access to plenty of material things. Jeff felt a need to give Brenda the lifestyle that she was accustomed to, but financially could not, in the early years of their marriage. Brenda had to convince Jeff that it was not his ability to provide material things that mattered to her, but that it was his love, authenticity and character that really mattered to her.

Obviously, Jeff's early experiences with the education system and confidence building were not the last words on his story. With the encouragement of his wife and other supportive family members, he completed his GED. He then went on to get an associate's, bachelor's and master's degrees! And again, at the time of our conversation, he was working on a second master's degree.

Even though Jeff and Brenda had grown up together, the couple realized there was a difference in knowing each other while growing up as friends and getting to know each other as adults in a marriage. Both still had a lot of learning to do about each other as husband and wife.

Jeff recalled that early on in their marriage, both of them were still immature and kind of selfish, wanting to meet their own individual interests instead of the needs of the couple - one of the big differences between dating and marriage. Jeff used his military intelligence skills and went to Brenda's Mom for some of her wisdom. Through his many conversations with her, Jeff recognized that they needed to identify each other's strengths in the marriage. He would take care of areas that were his strengths and Brenda would take care of areas that were hers. One of Brenda's Mom's golden nuggets to Jeff was to recognize that one of them was good with spending and therefore, the other had to be good with saving, putting money aside for un-expected needs in the family. As the couple used the approach to work from their strengths, some of their issues became much easier to navigate.

They reflected upon the numerous seasons experienced over their thirty-one plus years of marriage, newlyweds, without children, with young children, relocations as a military family, and now with adult children, a grandchild, and a new grand-baby on the way. Brenda saw as one of her strengths (and at times weaknesses) that she adores her family, her children and her husband, and she holds them very close. She recalled times when Jeff would plan surprise trips for the two of them to spend time together as a couple. This was tough for Brenda, because she always wanted the kids close by as she desired to be a total hands-on Mom. She had to learn how to balance her different roles, and to ensure she nurtured all of these roles; not only mother, grandmother and friend, but to continue to nurture her role of wife as well.

Brenda observed that effective communication between she and Jeff has been key. As their children grew up and were involved in numerous activities, coupled with Jeff's love of motorcycle trips, their schedules would get disconnected. At one point for a whole year, they did not have two weekends free because they had both really overcommitted themselves, and in the process overbooked their schedules. They had to admit they were not communicating effectively with each other as they were leaving no down-time in their schedules. They worked through this challenge by devising and sharing an electronic calendar to better coordinate upcoming events involving the family.

A serious 'underwater' season for Jeff and Brenda occurred when they experienced the loss of Jeff's mother and sister in the same year. Both of them died unexpectedly, during surgical procedures. It was as they grieved these losses that Brenda learned about GriefShare, a support ministry for people who have experienced the loss of a loved one. She attended first and then got Jeff to participate as well. Then within a year after Jeff's Mom and sister died, Brenda's Mom passed away. Brenda's grief engulfed her like total darkness. Both Jeff and Brenda found GriefShare to be a ministry that brought healing and a new lifeline for them. Brenda felt it was like striking a match to provide light in her darkness. GriefShare was so meaningful for the both of them that they agreed to become lead facilitators for their church's GriefShare Ministry, roles that they continued for over ten years.

Another challenge for this couple was that after the birth of their first child, Brenda suffered postpartum depression. Doctors didn't understand or readily diagnose postpartum depression at that time. She had a beautiful son and felt she should have been on top of the world, but instead she wanted to cry all the time. It was an overwhelming time for the marriage, as Brenda dealt with this depression and Jeff was preoccupied with figuring out his role as a father. They lived in Arizona at the time and Brenda talked to her pastor and first lady of their church. They helped her to really dig into her faith and stay prayerful. In addition, Brenda found a doctor who treated postpartum depression and prescribed her the right medication for a couple of months.

As Jeff reflected over the various seasons of being married, having children and grandchildren, he stated, "it was going from good to better to great!" Yet it doesn't mean the journey was easy for him. The most difficult part for him initially was fatherhood, because his parents separated very early in his life. So, he did not have a great example of fatherhood. He found himself unsure of what to do or be when his son was born. But through his faith he began to look to the scriptures for insight. He did not want his son to experience the things that he had gone through. So, he made a concerted effort to make his son's childhood as enjoyable as possible. When their daughter was born, Jeff was more comfortable in his own skin as a father.

And becoming a grandparent was when things became great as he got all of the joys without the parenting rules that go along with raising children.

Brenda noted she is very extroverted and loves people, but she explained she can also be extremely shy sometimes. According to Jeff, it was quite a revelation to him in that moment of the interview, that his wife was shy. He humorously remembered a train trip they took from Boston to Washington, DC. He felt before they got to Washington, Brenda had held a meeting of the United Nations, because she had conversed with every person she could on the train! So, Brenda's reported shyness just shows that partners can keep learning more about each other even after thirty-one years of marriage.

With the stories of challenges Jeff and Brenda shared, they pointed to their faith in God as their key to being overcomers. Without it they would never have conquered challenges such as being financially strapped, dealing with health issues, marital issues, children and school issues, and all of the common struggles that families go through. Jeff noted, "While today it may look as if they never had any struggle, it was faith that let them persevere through every challenge in every season. And it's such a wonderful blessing to preach and share your faith with your family and see the impact it is having in their lives!"

Brenda and Jeff are continuing to change and grow…but they are navigating those changes together. From their experience they point to the importance of taking time to understand your spouse's beliefs, morals and perspectives. What has been a big success for this couple is that they get behind each other's dreams. For example, Jeff shared that he tries to understand where Brenda wants to go in ministry, or her career or as a mother and grandmother. He then tries to support her as much as he possibly can with the stance that she takes; Brenda in turn is also supportive of Jeff's goals and his roles.

Rev. Jeff and Brenda Gaines beautifully illustrated the fact that marriage has many different seasons and how a couple can work through the seasons together. Over all the changes in their lives, their constant has been having God and each other. Today, Jeff and Brenda are living their best lives, building their dream home in Florida, working together in BG Consulting Services LLC and continuing to be God's salt and light through their giving and serving others!!

NOTE: Jeff and Brenda shared a special note about the value of GriefShare. While GriefShare is understandably a 'club' no one wants to be a part of, it is a ministry that can help you when you have lost someone very close to you, or conversely, if you have lost someone very important to you that you did not have a good relationship with, and this may cause you to grieve very hard. When it's a suicide, or sudden death, or a murder, it can bring out rage and anger because you don't understand it. In GriefShare, you will be a part of a group that can relate to what you're going through and provide you support. During the sessions you watch specific videos about the process of grief and then get to talk as a group about what you are experiencing and feeling. Jeff and Brenda invite anyone needing grief support to go to www. griefshare.org to locate a GriefShare group near them.

REFLECTIONS FOR YOU:

1. If you are married, how would you describe this season of your relationship?

2. What perspectives did you gain from Jeff & Brenda's story?

3. What is one small step that you could begin taking this week to enrich your marriage?

4. What did you learn about coping with grief? Are you dealing with any grief where you could use support?

YOUR MINDSET MATTERS - JOSEPH 'JOE' ALEXANDER

Do not be anxious about anything, but in everything by prayer and supplication with thanksgiving let your requests be made known to God. And the peace of God, which surpasses all understanding, will guard your hearts and your minds in Christ Jesus. (Philippians 4:6-7)

It is not uncommon that we hear about hardship and heaviness when someone we know, or the media shows stories of people going through life's most difficult seasons. When you converse with someone who is going through or has been through a very difficult season of life, you may observe a mindset where the person is consumed by his or her challenges or they are overwhelmed by their hardships as too much to bear. They may display a loss of hope, a focus on how long they have faced the difficulty, or even how much harder their trial is in comparison to others. These scenarios prompt the questions, when facing storms in life, what can make a difference? Does your mindset matter? In other words, does your mindset play a role in how you manage your personal and spiritual relationships when facing storms in your life?

Would we hear anything different from a person walking through a season of major challenges whose faith in God permeates his mindset and actions? Let's see as we walk along with Joseph 'Joe' Alexander Jr.

Joe was born in Valdosta, GA and shortly after his birth, his father joined the Air Force. The Alexanders became a military family with Joe becoming the eldest of six children. The family had the opportunity to live in Alabama, Texas, Mississippi, Florida and Northern Japan, where Joe began high school. After an assignment in Missouri, where his dad retired, Joe finished high school and went to college.

After graduating from college, Joe chose the Army for his career, which afforded him further opportunities to see the world. The various moves and travel provided Joe a different lens with which to look at the world. His growing up years and career gave him the opportunity to see a lot of different situations and to look at them from different perspectives.

His core values and foundation, instilled in him by his parents were first, faith in God, and then to have a personal relationship with Him. Joe's core value of faith is undergirded by values of education, dedication and service. Given his core values, the many relocations and diversity of experiences, what was the common theme of Joe's journey? Flexibility. He came to understand his changing environments. And Joe gleaned a spiritual connotation to his flexibility. Joe believed that we are all in a perpetual state of growth and in our spiritual life we need to be prepared to hear what God has in store for us and where he is leading us. That requires us to be flexible to join Him in accomplishing His will. Joe pointed out that the Bible shows the need for flexibility through leaders in the Bible such as Moses, Paul or the 12 apostles, none of whom originally set out to do the things God called them to do.

On the specific topic of whether one's mindset matters, Joe again underscored his core value of having faith and knowing that you are not alone. His perspective was that no matter what is before you to accomplish, God is there. We prepare through educating ourselves on what we're trying to accomplish, then put in the hard work and dedication required. Joe adds a significant next step, asking what is the benefit of your goal? Will it only benefit you? Will it benefit others? Is it going to glorify God? After you've educated yourself, dedicated yourself to the task and determined the benefit and how it's going to work. Then Joe again noted how critical it is to be flexible. Chiefly, it's being willing to adapt to what God wants us to do.

Joe felt that we should examine our mindset around success. He had witnessed people who look at the success of others and try to mimic or model that same success in their own lives. Just as our relationship with Christ is a very personal thing, Joe views success just the same way. He stated explicitly, "God is not a cookie cutter God who provides the same blessings to you as He does to me generically. The blessings may be similar, but how he provides the blessings and why He provides them may be altogether different." Joe was clear; we can adopt a mindset that God's blessings for us are the ones He intends for us.

Joe is immersed in his faith during tough trials and challenges. At the time of our conversation, Joe was actually in the midst of two tough situations. His then 10-year-old granddaughter, Julia, had been diagnosed with a malignant brain tumor. In fact, she had already undergone three major surgeries and several secondary procedures over the 18-month period since her diagnosis. Yet Joe noted that his granddaughter continues to go to school, and the family had recently experienced one of the most joyful things. Julia had accepted Christ and was baptized. He described the experience of watching his granddaughter go through this major health challenge and her strength and spiritual growth and dedication as rewarding.

The second challenge that Joe and his family were facing at the time, was that his father, who is a minister, had Alzheimer's disease and was moved to a Veterans home. His mother, who was supporting him, was then living alone. Joe was grappling with the delicate balance of providing support to his father and his mother, while allowing his mother to maintain some independence while she still could.

The pain of both situations Joe described could be devastating or paralyzing. How was he coping with these challenges? The same way he has dealt with other challenges that he has faced in the past, and that is to pray and look to God. He admitted the greatest challenge is that in these circumstances, all he could do was step back and accept that he could only be a support to his family. By his nature, Joe, a problem solver, wanted to provide a solution. Through prayer, Joe recognized he was in a different role. Instead of a problem solver, he had to be in the role of supporter.

Did Joe get discouraged sometimes when his prayers were not answered as quickly as he wanted or with the exact answer that he wanted? Yes. But he understood then and still does, that he is not in control - God is. His foundation always leads him back to get on his knees and pray, not just daily, but multiple times a day, turning the circumstances over to the Lord and seeking what the Lord would have him to do in the situation. From the standpoint of Joe's granddaughter, he knew that he and his wife as well as other family members were called to just back up his son and daughter-in-law, supporting Julia and seeing her through this. From the standpoint of his father and mother, Joe came to understand they were dealing with Alzheimer's, a debilitating disease. Joe felt called to continue to love his father and to remember that he was safe, and to continue to pray for him and his well-being. And he felt called to also pray for his mother and for peace for both of his parents. Joe's father passed away nearly four years ago, and his mother now lives with him and his wife, Kathy.

The major lesson that Joe has taken from being in the midst of this challenging season was to continue to communicate and walk with the Lord. Joe remembers that God desires to be in a personal relationship with us and he wants to maintain that loving, personal relationship with the Lord.

What is Joe most looking forward to in the future? His answer was telling. Joe was looking forward to what God has in store, to be obedient and to do what God has intended for him. Obviously, he wanted things to go well and for his trials to end, but Joe's mindset was to trust that God was strengthening him through his trials to become a better person. Joe felt nudged to continue to be active in teaching Bible study classes and doing his own independent Bible study at home. He planned to continue to share the Word of God as often as he could, not necessarily through quoting scriptures, but through what he called 'lifestyle evangelism' which meant that he walks or carries himself in a faith-filled manner.

Joe's perspective was that we should always be in a perpetual state of growth because God has some amazing things for us to do, some large, some small, but if we accept what he calls us to do, it's going to bring Him glory. Joe's mindset matters. His lens in life, whether considering his family, his success, his day-to-day walk, major trials or his future plans, remains focused on trusting God, His wisdom and His will.

UPDATE: A praise report on Joe's granddaughter, Julia. Although the remainder of Julia's tumor is inoperable, it is dormant. She is now 15 years old and is a high school honor roll student!

REFLECTIONS FOR YOU:

1. What were your personal takeaways from reading Joe's story?

2. Have you ever had to surrender your role as 'problem solver' and instead just provide support?

3. What insights from Joe can help you to adjust your mindset to cope with trials in your life?

LEAPING OVER LIMITING BELIEFS - REV. ALAN HARRIS

For nothing will be impossible with God. (Luke 1:37)

When students are in high school, they are often asked, what do you want to be or do? They have dreams for their future, maybe even with the idea in mind of attending a particular college to prepare to reach their dreams. But what happens if a guidance counselor tells a student that based on their GPA, he has concluded that the student should look into trade schools or some other possibility because the guidance counselor doesn't think the student is college material?

You too may have gotten a message earlier in life from a guidance counselor, teacher, parent, family friend or someone of influence, on what you could or could not do. What might such a declaration do to the dreams and hopes of a student? It's either something that the student accepts as fact, or it could be viewed as an opinion, allowing one to still move forward without letting the limiting beliefs stop them.

In high school, Rev. Alan Harris had a guidance counselor express those limiting beliefs to him, that he should look into trade schools or some other possibility because he didn't think he was college material. We'll see what unfolds. Rev. Harris is an ordained minister of the Gospel. A native of St Louis, Missouri, he began his preaching ministry at the age of 19 and has served in full time ministry since he was 22 years old. Rev. Harris describes himself as an introvert who likes to observe, yet one of his favorite aspects of ministry is interacting with and being around people, enjoying making them laugh. He is an avid sports fan and also loves traveling, reading and watching movies.

Rev. Harris is the Associate Pastor of Student Ministries at Antioch Baptist Church in Fairfax Station, VA. He and his wife Joy have a beloved son, Isaiah. From his teenage years, Rev. Harris knew that he wanted a family, and felt that God created him to be a 'family guy.' It was always his preference to get married young, and God granted that wish by allowing him to get married at 24. And he and his wife became parents to their son when he was 29. Whether he had pursued higher education or not, Rev. Harris' life had been blessed to this point. He was a gifted, anointed preacher, and he and his beautiful family were inspiring and loved members of the Antioch church community.

As is the case for many people, life was moving along happily and with some predictability when a life-changing challenge occurred. For Rev. Harris it happened in 2009. On a Wednesday morning as he was getting ready for work, his cell phone rang. He saw that it was his aunt in St Louis calling. He did not answer as he continued getting ready for work. When his mom called thirty seconds later, he figured something was going on and answered the phone. His mom told him that his grandmother had gone into cardiac arrest and was at the hospital. Rev. Harris immediately headed to his mother's house which was a twenty-minute drive. He prayed during the drive that God would sustain and revive his grandmother.

When he got to his mom's house, he learned that his

grandmother didn't make it. Rev Harris, a grandmother's boy, was devastated and shocked. They had a very, very close and strong relationship and would talk three or four days a week on the phone for 50-60 minutes. And either she would visit him in Virginia, or he would go home to St Louis to see her every year. One of the things about his grandmother's passing that ate away at him for a long time was that their last conversation was not a usual lengthy one. It was very brief because he had something else to do and he told her he would call her back. After a few days, he still had not called her back and the following Wednesday was when God took her home.

How did Rev. Harris persevere during such a life-changing loss? There were three key things that got him through this most difficult period in his life. One was prayer. As a minister, he was accustomed to devoting a lot of time in prayer for others. However, the pain from losing his grandmother was so deep that it revitalized and re-energized his personal prayer life. He was learning to pray for himself as well as just being honest with God and sharing his feelings of pain and not understanding, and even expressing some feelings of anger towards Him for taking his grandmother unannounced.

A second key was getting into the Word. Not looking to find his next sermon or bible study, Rev. Harris just feasted on God's Word and felt it minister to him at his point of need. The third key that helped him endure the loss was the support of his wife, Joy. She was there whether lending her ear when he wanted to talk or lending her shoulder when he needed to cry. She truly showed up as his best friend during this tremendous loss.

Speaking directly to the impact of his faith on dealing with the loss, Rev. Harris recalled his grandmother saying, 'Life is difficult enough with God, so I don't understand how some people can make it through without God.' Rev. Harris' pain and depth of loss allowed him to extract the essence of her words. His faith let him know that there is purpose for what we go through, that God is not only aware of our pain, but He is sensitive to, and heals our pain. And most importantly, his faith let him know that because his grandmother was also a believer, he would see her again. So, Rev. Harris grieved, but he was also able to love and have hope in the midst of his grief.

As our conversation took place near the end of the year, Rev. Harris also shared what he does to prepare himself for a new year. He acknowledged the importance of taking some time to really reflect upon the year that God has brought us through, and to discover what God is requiring of us, asking us to do differently, and to do better in the New Year. Rev. Harris gave a couple of key illustrations of where we need to check our mindsets as we move into a new year. He heard a pastor say once, "not only can our past mistakes hinder us from doing great things in the future, but sometimes our past achievements can hinder us from doing great things in the future as well." In other words, Rev. Harris noted in some cases that when we do achieve significant goals we have set for ourselves, we put things on cruise control, dwelling on what we've already done. We can create limiting beliefs ourselves about what we can or cannot still do.

Instead, Rev. Harris recommends we enter a new year knowing that we are stewards of everything. He asks himself, "how can I be a better steward of everything that God has given me as I go into this New Year? How can I be a better steward as it relates to time, as it relates to my temple?" Rev Harris modeled the mentality of the Apostle Paul when he said, "forgetting those things which lie behind..." that is to say, don't look back, but keep your eyes focused on the future knowing that there are goals, and there are things that God wants to do in you and through you.

Another pointed observation about our mindset going into a New Year, was with respect to forgiveness. We need to remind ourselves that we serve a God who is forgiving. If God forgives us of our sins, then we need to forgive ourselves and keep marching forward to the great things that God has in store for us. Equally important, Rev. Harris emphasized the issue of being unforgiving towards others. He himself had been challenged and had to grow through the issue of unforgiveness. He was reminded that we are most like Christ when we forgive people who do not deserve our forgiveness. When Rev. Harris has thought of all the times that Christ has forgiven and understood him, he asks himself, "how can I not be forgiving to those who have hurt or offended me?"

Rev. Harris understood the difficulty when people ask, "is it really possible to forgive and forget?" It's the forgetting part that stops some from moving forward. He believes that God causes us to forgive wholeheartedly. And at the same time, He calls us to use sound judgment. Rev. Harris used an example to buttress the point. If he had a friend and the friend stabs him, he's going to forgive the friend. But if he sees that friend with that same knife, will he walk close to that friend? Probably not. While he will forgive, his judgment and discernment will guide how he moves forward with that person. Simply stated, we can be forgiving and still walk with wisdom.

What powerful insights to take into a new year, but even to take into a new month or a new week! We can dwell too much on past mistakes or accomplishments, instead of seeking God's guidance for what lies ahead and what He wants to do to and through us. And secondly, there is great value in being forgiving of ourselves and of others, for we are most like Christ when we do.

Which effect did the limiting beliefs of Rev. Harris' high school guidance counselor ultimately have on him? Did he hold to what the counselor said as fact and pursue an alternative to college? Or did he take the counselor's view as an opinion and leap over the limiting beliefs?

After graduating from high school, Rev. Harris went on to obtain his Bachelor of Arts in Biblical Studies from Washington Bible College. And he did not stop there. His hunger and desire to be enriched intellectually and spiritually led him to matriculate at Southern Seminary, where he obtained his Master of Divinity Degree realizing leaders must continue to grow. It took him about six years to complete his masters as his son was born while he was working on his graduate degree.

And Rev. Harris still did not stop there. When he began his master's study, his goal was to complete it and be finished with education. But during the fourth or fifth year of working on his masters, the Lord led him to pursue a doctorate! At the time of our interview, Rev. Harris had completed the first year of his doctoral program in Strategic Leadership. He is on target to graduate with his doctorate in the spring of 2022.

Rev. Harris is a stellar example of leaping over limiting beliefs! He took the guidance counselor's feedback as an opinion and did not let those beliefs become an obstacle to reaching his full potential. He models being God-led and determined, showing excellence in his roles as a husband and father, in his pursuit of education, and his anointing in ministry.

He has been afforded the opportunity to preach in Toronto, Austria, Kenya and Haiti. Rev. Alan Harris is dedicated to speaking the good news of Jesus Christ to everyone he comes in contact with, believing the gospel is to be heard at the ends of the earth.

REFLECTIONS FOR YOU:

1. In what ways can you personally relate to Rev Harris' story?

2. What limiting beliefs do you need to leap over?

3. What steps do you take to prepare yourself for a new year? What steps could be even more helpful to you?

CHAPTER TWO

OVERCOMING IN CAREER MATTERS

GIFTED TO SERVE THROUGH MUSIC – CURTIS TAYLOR SR.

My heart, O God, is steadfast, my heart is steadfast; I will sing and make music. (Psalm 57:7)

Do you have a gift, or have you ever longed to be gifted through music? Visualize growing up in a family where your Mom, Dad, siblings and you are all gifted musically. That is Curtis Taylor Sr's story. Growing up in South Carolina, his father was the band master at the local high school (Tomlinson High in Kingstree, South Carolina) his mother was an educator and lyric soprano. His sister was a jazz singer and composer, and his brother was a music producer. There was always music in their home. Curtis was taught to play piano and various other instruments at a very early age by his father. As more of Curtis' life unfolds below, it will be interesting to see if music remained an integral part of his life.

Curtis grew up in the church, accepted Christ at age 12, and his first values started to form there within the church and his home where the heavy emphasis on music continued and his personal love of music began to grow. When Curtis graduated from high school, he was faced with the choice of attending Morehouse College, a great university, or South Carolina State University. But once his dad took him to a football game at South Carolina State and he heard the Marching 101 Band, his decision was made. Curtis told his dad, "I've got to play in this band!" He did attend South Carolina State and eventually became the student director of the Marching 101 Band. At the same time, Curtis and friends also had a side band called The Soul Agents, an R&B group that played at various functions.

The Soul Agents even had the opportunity to audition for and be selected to play with James Brown (The Godfather of Soul) for about seven months! What was one of his observations of the Godfather of Soul? Curtis shared that James Brown was a stickler for being on time. If one was late for rehearsal or late for a performance, they were fined profusely. James Brown was at the peak of his career at this time. Curtis observed how he ran his business in a very professional manner, and as a college student just getting started in life, Curtis was able to learn valuable lessons from James Brown.

While at South Carolina State, Curtis completed four years of Army Reserve Officers Training Corps (ROTC) and would later serve as an Army officer. While still in college, Curtis' personal life also took a very positive turn. There he 'chased' his wife, the former Abigail "Abby" Brown. He recognized that Abby had lots of choices of boyfriends, but fortunately, he held her interest. (Note: At the time of our discussion, Curtis and Abby had been married over 43 years with three adult sons, two daughters-in-law and seven grandchildren.)

Curtis graduated with a bachelor's degree in music. Before graduating from college, he received an invitation to audition for a spot at the prestigious Cornell University's Graduate School of Music. Upon graduation from South Carolina State, he was granted a delayed entry into the military to pursue a graduate music program. What an experience from the onset his journey at Cornell University turned out to be. When he arrived from South Carolina for the audition, one of the committee members evaluating new candidates asked if he was going to play a jazz tune. Really? There seemed to be some type of assumption there. But Curtis answered no, that he would be playing the selection, Les Funerailles, S, 173 No 7. Curtis' mentor, Mr. Eugene Pinson, suggested the masterful composition for his audition to show his musical dexterity. Curtis observed the committee members' look of surprise that he, an African American youth from South Carolina State University, even knew how to pronounce this selection by Franz Liszt. Curtis played the entire score of over 29 pages of sheet music from memory, which really impressed the committee. He received a full scholarship for Cornell University's Master's in Music program!

The graduate program was not easy, but Curtis persevered. His thesis (a stylistic comparative analysis of two recordings by Duke Ellington) was developed into a full-blown Broadway musical entitled 'Cotton Club Revue!' Before graduation from Cornell, Curtis faced a major hurdle, when he was told by professors that he had to pass a foreign language proficiency exam before his degree could be awarded. Curtis had not been made aware of this requirement earlier in the program, but God was watching over him and sent him an angel.

After the meeting, one of the professors pulled Curtis aside and offered to tutor him in a foreign language. The professor met with him every day for about six weeks in a noisy pub across the street from the university. Curtis scored in the 95th percentile on his foreign language proficiency exam, and this indicated just how effective the tutoring had been. Curtis attributed it all to God, sending an angel as his tutor, because he knew if he had not passed the exam, he would not have graduated.

Curtis became the first African American to receive a Master of Music Degree from Cornell University! His fortitude and perseverance opened the door to opportunities at Cornell for other African American music students. Armed with a master's degree in Music Theory and Composition, Curtis began his military career as an officer in the United States Army.

Knowing Curtis, Abby and their beautiful family, during our conversation, it was not apparent that the family had walked through any difficult seasons as their children grew up. Curtis had served as an Army officer for 26 years. He was very proud to serve, yet it came with some significant challenges to his family life. They moved 11 times in 26 years, and each one of those moves was difficult - particularly in the later years of his career when the moves became every two years. Curtis noted; "the more successful you are in the military, the more frequently you are required to move."

A few moves and separations from his family were particularly challenging. He once had an assignment to move to Korea for two years without his family. Abby and their one son at the time, remained in South Carolina where she took the full responsibility for raising their son and maintaining their home. Another separation came when Curtis became a battalion commander and was in Baltimore for two years. They made the decision for her and their sons to remain in

Virginia so their oldest son could graduate from high school there. While it allowed stability for their son in his last year of high school, it was a tough time for them all enduring another family separation. The third example was when Curtis went to brigade command and the family moved to Indianapolis, but at the time his middle son was approaching 11th grade. He had to be pulled out of the 11th grade and it took almost a year for him to get adjusted to a new school, make new friends and adapt to the environment in Indiana.

One of the very stressful dimensions of this challenging season was when they faced a juncture where they were about to own three houses - yes three. They had the new house that they were buying in Northern Virginia and two on the market: one in South Carolina and one in Indiana. With three kids and close to having three mortgages at once, the Taylors could have easily been on the verge of bankruptcy. But God sent angels again. Through God's grace, Curtis ran into a military colleague who agreed to rent their house in Indianapolis and then even agreed to sell the house for them, wow! Shortly after that, the house in South Carolina sold and they were able to settle in Virginia with one mortgage, whew! One of the other challenges of their frequent military moves, all too common with military spouses, was the inability for Abby to establish her career. Fortunately, once they settled in Northern Virginia, Abby got to pursue a fulfilling career as a speech pathologist and director of speech pathology in Fairfax County.

Curtis reflected on having a great military career, great experiences and travel for his family, but admittedly it came with a lot of challenges. He decided to retire when he did because he wanted more stability for his youngest son as he approached high school, and for Abby to be able to build the career she desired. Curtis and his family relied on their faith to get them through the challenges as they moved over and over again. It was lots and lots of prayer, faith in God and perseverance. Curtis has seen what happens when you keep the faith, as he shared for example, how the Lord spared them having three mortgages. Albeit with much human frustration and doubt, they never lost faith that somehow, they were going to be okay, that God would take care of them. They just knew that God had brought them too far to let them fail.

At the time of our interview, still keeping his faith strong, Curtis was an accomplished corporate executive director of government contracts for Advanced Systems Development Inc. In 2016, he enjoyed working with his sons, Curtis Jr and Richard, as they established an information technology services company, TIS Solutions.

With his variety of roles as a Christian, military leader, husband, and parent, over the years Curtis has found himself as a go-to person when others are grappling with life challenges. What's a general piece of advice he gives to someone who is facing a challenging season? Stay close to God. Don't stray. Find a professional to talk to or talk to your family and friends. Most importantly, don't go through your trials alone. "Get some support," Curtis emphasized, and he continued to practice reaching out to his own close knit support system whenever he was going through life's trials.

When Curtis reflected on the year gone by, he was clear that his top four priorities were unchanged; God, then family, then work and then pleasure. Curtis shared a few noteworthy tips on keeping a healthy, strong marriage for over 43 years. First, Curtis believes it is important to always treat your marriage as though you just got married. Keep it fresh and keep dating each other. Second, he noted the need for mutual respect in the marriage, not taking actions without each other's mutual agreement and respect. Lastly Curtis mentioned the importance of sharing a strong faith in God and how they have together made that a foundation of their marriage.

Did Curtis keep his love and passion for music over all the years? Indeed, he did! During a military assignment while living in Heidelberg, Germany, he worked with the Army community to re-create the magic of a musical he had created while in college. The Cotton Club Review toured and was well received in communities throughout Germany. In the midst of his other professional ventures, Curtis continued to be an accomplished pianist, vocalist and music arranger. In addition, he was the director of the music ministry in his church, directing the activities of five choirs and personally directing a gospel choir, men's ensemble and mass choir for many years of church services and area-wide special events. He has led a Christian music ministry trip throughout Austria with an ensemble of choir members. He led a gospel & jazz quintet, Curtis Taylor Quintet (CTQ), where he also played keyboards during performances at numerous community outreach and social venues throughout the Washington DC metro region.

Curtis Taylor went home to glory in December of 2020 and is sorely missed by his family and all who were blessed to know him. For all of his days, Curtis remained passionate about serving God through his gift of music. He took care of his family as a responsible, loving husband, father and grandfather. For these reasons and for the way he fed souls throughout the community with God's love, he will always be remembered.

REFLECTIONS FOR YOU:

1. What new personal insights did you gain from Curtis' story?

2. What have you been passionate about over many years and how do you keep that passion alive?

3. Have you been in a difficult situation when a solution suddenly appeared? What did you attribute the solution to?

THE KEY TO FINDING CONTENTMENT – DALE FLETCHER

I am not saying this because I am in need, for I have learned to be content whatever the circumstances. I know what it is to be in need, and I know what it is to have plenty. I have learned the secret of being content in any and every situation, whether well fed or hungry, whether living in plenty or in want. I can do all this through him who gives me strength. (Philippians 4:11-13)

If you were asked, "what does contentment mean to you?", how would you define it? Below are a sample of actual responses to this question asked on social media:

- Contentment is being comfortable with who I am and whose I am knowing that with Him all things are possible.
- When I do something for myself, living simply and trusting God's grace and provisions for my life.
- Contentment is walking away from my job and returning home to care for my 95-year-old mom who has dementia.
- Living a simple life, eating less, picking one skill and becoming a master in your career.
- Contentment is peace with God and your surroundings, your relationships and environment.
- Making sure the bills are paid and the kids are taken care of and not feeling guilty.

- Contentment is knowing that I am loved unconditionally by God and there is nothing I can do to make Him stop.

Finding contentment is a worthwhile exploration for us, no matter what season of life we are in. In a wide-ranging discussion with a fellow believer in Christ, Dale Fletcher, he shared some insights on his finding contentment, and he shared so much more about what drives his life and how he wants to show up in the world. You will easily see where contentment fits in. Here's his story.

Dale Fletcher grew up in a military family, relocating every two to three years due to his father's military assignments. The family lived in Georgia, Kansas, Idaho, Washington State, and Alaska as Dale grew up. Dale humorously recalled being new to his eighth-grade class in Georgia, having just moved to Georgia from Alaska. He convinced his fellow students that in Alaska, he had lived in an igloo and attended school in an igloo. When Dale finished high school, he attended the U. S. Army Military Academy at West Point and became an Army officer which allowed him to continue to travel the world, relocating every few years due to his military assignments.

Dale's life encompasses several core values. First and foremost is his desire that his Christian faith, his relationship with God and biblical truth guides how he lives and the choices he makes. Family is next; he and his wife Janice, fostering family bonds and cohesion with their four adult children, their siblings, nieces and nephews, and now new grandson, Judah.

And lastly, Dale values wellness of spirit, mind and body as he believes our personal health and well-being is a resource that enables us to live life in a way that glorifies God. As a result, Dale does not underestimate the significance of caring for his health the best way he can.

Looking back, one of Dale's most impactful memories is pertinent to his valuing personal health and wellness. During Dale's Army career, in the mid-80s, he had a wonderful opportunity to be the first course director of the master fitness trainer course at the Army Fitness School. For three years, he was responsible for putting together the curriculum and the instructors for a four-week program to lead and teach Army Master Fitness Trainers to conduct fitness programming Army-wide. And Dale's program was more physiologically sound than what had been done with the training before. The training made a difference in the lives of many. While the curriculum has been updated as needed over the years, it is highly memorable and satisfying for Dale to know that he led the initial team and curriculum development that has subsequently trained over 10,000 Master Fitness Trainers!

Today one of the hats Dale wears is the head of a ministry called Faith & Health Connection. How did he get there? Dale was working at the Harris YMCA in Charlotte, North Carolina as a Wellness Director. But in 2005, he felt God calling Him to do something different, and he subsequently left that position. You see, during Dale's work at the YMCA, he had exposure to the concept of health coaching and being a coach, which included the empowerment of people to make decisions and choices, and helping them discover their own solutions, specifically regarding their health and their health shortcomings. As Dale was employed at a YMCA, a Christian organization, he had a vision to possibly train a cadre of individuals and call them spirit, mind & body health coaches. Dale had been trained in a curriculum that could be modified and used in the YMCA setting, but his vision never fully materialized. Dale felt God calling him to go deeper in this area. The need for a mechanism to go deeper in this pursuit led Dale to establish Faith and Health Connection ministry which during our conversation in 2017 was already 10 years old! The ministry's mission statement is '*Teaching Biblical Truths for Health and Wholeness.*'

Dale's perspective on wholeness is that we will not be completely whole until we get to heaven someday. We have a body, a soul and personality that will be imperfect on this side of heaven. Although we will not be perfectly well or whole until we get to heaven, we can have a goal to attain the greatest degree of wholeness that we can. And the Faith and Health Connection Ministry teaches biblical principles on how to do that. For Christians, we are impacted by the Holy Spirit that lives within us and we can steadily become more like Jesus as we live.

Through the Faith and Health Connection Ministry, Dale created a bible study that went from a two to four to now a ten-week published bible study, called 'Pathway 2 Wholeness.' This bible study is a part of the Faith and Health Ambassadors Course that Dale has run for the last six years, training close to 120 ambassadors. This course along with a 600+ page website makes up the Faith and Health Connection Ministry. The ministry website is very popular, in some months having over 40,000 people visit the site.

As Dale discussed his life's journey, he opened up about a particularly challenging situation he faced and how he persevered through it. In 2006, Dale was diagnosed with prostate cancer and had a choice to make on how he was going to handle it. Three weeks before he was scheduled to have a prostatectomy, Dale had what he thought was extreme laryngitis. However, he was referred to an ENT specialist and learned that he had a paralyzed vocal cord. Dale was certain that nothing happens in isolation to the mind, body and spirit. He felt without a doubt that the stress associated with the diagnosis of prostate cancer had manifested itself also through a paralyzed vocal cord. Dale immediately turned to God to manage the stressors in his life. He recalled a blog post he wrote in that period. It stated: "This series of events has brought me even closer to God for sure. I've been reading more about how God heals people. I have become very intentional to be in His presence, and to be as close to Him as possible. It's during times like this that I have experienced the loving touch of God. I have a choice; free will to turn to God and be with Him more or to turn away from Him and try to do this on my own. I've chosen the first path and I know I have been better off for it." Dale had already decided before the health challenge that as the stressors of life come at him, he would turn to his faith. When Dale faced his health trials, he leaned into God and to His promises. He was not afraid, he trusted God and prayed that His will would be done, and he rested in that space.

Looking further into Dale's faith walk, he discussed finding contentment. He believes it is first about trusting God. The key to trusting God is knowing God and that His Word, the Bible is truth. Through the truth of the Bible, he is guided to live a life that has fruit because our purpose is to glorify God in this life. For Dale, glorifying God has become the filter through which he tries to make the choices on how to respond to stressors and storms in life.

Here's how Dale defined contentment: "Living a life of peace, an absence of anxiousness, the absence of worry, a deep inner peace." When we are at peace, we are satisfied, including when everything is not as we want it to be. In the Bible, Philippians 4:11, Paul says I have learned in whatever situation I am, to be content. Dale recognized Paul's contentment came from the surrender of his life and his will to Christ. Dale then revealed his key to finding contentment this way, "Living a life surrendered to God's ways and to Him. In our weakness, it is actually Jesus, His power, the Spirit of God that is manifested. He empowers us to speak and respond to life's storms and stressors in ways that encourage and give hope to others."

At the end of our discussion, Dale answered one last question: what story do you want your life to tell? He stated he is still a work in progress, but his heart's desire is for people to see that he's a man who loves God and desires to live life in a way that brings glory to Him. He understands that the way to glorify God is to live by the power of the Holy Spirit, producing a lot of fruit in his life. He wants his life story to show that he loved others in ways that were practical and tangible, that he demonstrated a strong belief and trust in God in a way that brought hope and encouragement to others and that he made a difference in the lives of others. Dale Fletcher's life does indeed tell that story. To God be the glory!!

REFLECTIONS FOR YOU:

1. What perspectives can you take from Dale's story for your life?

2. What is your key to finding contentment?

3. How have you responded when God has nudged you in a new direction?

ONE DOOR CLOSES. ANOTHER DOOR OPENS – KEITHA V. JOHNSON

Ask and it will be given to you; seek and you will find; knock and the door will be opened to you. For everyone who asks receives; the one who seeks finds; and to the one who knocks, the door will be opened. (Matthew 7: 7-8)

Have you ever had the experience where you feel settled and intend to 'stay put' where you are? It could be in a job, a relationship, a location, financial status, state of health or otherwise. Sometimes we can lose ourselves in the familiar. In other words, we can become so comfortable with the status quo that we cannot see the untapped potential for growth or enrichment if we make some changes in our lives. The irony is we may not be so satisfied with the status quo, but because we are so accustomed to it, we stay where we are. But sometimes a door unexpectedly closes, and we have no choice but to move on.

Keitha V. Johnson shared her story of working successfully in her military career until a day came when the door on that career closed. But first, here's a bit of her background. Keitha grew up in Phenix City, Alabama, with a loving mother and father, as the middle child with an older sister and younger brother. She saw herself as a peacemaker of sorts, and she recalls using humor to keep harmony between her and her siblings. Keitha however noted that her Mom may have had other descriptions of her than peacemaker. She enjoyed school and had a great love of learning. She grew up in the church and learned to love to serve the Lord. She felt from early on that her purpose was to go out and put the talents God had given her to the very best use. She felt a pressing need to continue to discover her talents throughout her life and employ them to the best of her ability. Her core values that still drive her life today are honesty, loyalty and dedication.

Keitha received her undergraduate education at the University of Alabama, where she was commissioned as a Second Lieutenant in the Army. Over the course of Keitha serving in the Army, she had a variety of jobs and moved to lots of different assignments stateside and abroad. She made close friends who became like family over the years. Keitha served well -and the Army served Keitha well- because she became familiar with all of the different functions from administration to intelligence to operations, civil affairs, command and control and resource management. She recognized that the opportunities she was afforded, the people she met and the relationships all combined, allowed her to be in the right place at the right time to serve God as she was doing at the time of our conversation. How well prepared she was in the Army for what God had in store for her a bit later!

When Keitha was a Major in the Army, eligible for promotion to Lieutenant Colonel, she thought her record was good enough and that she would be on the promotion list. However, she was not selected for promotion. The day before the results were announced publicly to the Army, her boss, Lieutenant Colonel Woody Collins, called her into his office. He let her know that she had not been selected for promotion. He was empathetic. He told her that she was a good soldier and had done a good job and had a good career. He also told her not to be discouraged because a lot of her peers would get promoted. But of course, Keitha felt disappointed; who wouldn't? And it did discourage her that her peers were selected and she was not, including members whom she had gone through her entire Army career with. Keitha felt really bad.

However, the next statement her boss said really pierced through to her core. He said to her; "You have a purpose. And your purpose has to be fulfilled. You've just got to go out and do it." Wow! Those words made Keitha's mind fall back to God's Word and she responded: "I know God has a plan for my life, even if part of that plan is my not becoming a Lieutenant Colonel in the Army." Keitha comprehended that being a Lieutenant Colonel was not the know all, be all of her life. And she could not let this break her. At the time she did not know what God's plan was, but she knew she had to settle herself down and not focus solely on a position or title that she did not obtain.

Keitha always had a saying, "I was Keitha before I entered the military and I'm going to be Keitha whenever I leave, no matter what." Keitha began to go back to scriptures, the things that she knew God had promised. Not getting promoted would mean she would have to retire from the Army sooner than she had planned. But she knew God had something for her and she just had to be patient, work through this circumstance. and not worry about what others thought of her not getting promoted.

One of Keitha's biggest lessons at the time was that she could not control, nor could any of us control what people think of us. She put it this way, "When we live worrying about what others will think or say, we stifle ourselves. It's far more important to keep our focus on God and to be true to what God leads us to do." So, what was next for Keitha? Just around the bend for her were two new roles.

Once Keitha came to terms with the discomforting news that the door was closing to what she desired in the Army, she made a decision to pursue work as a comedian. How did the comedy come about? From Keitha's childhood, she was naturally funny. As early as third or fourth grade, after school each day, Keitha's antics would have a group of kids gathered around her as she waited for her sister. Even singing her name – 'Keitha Vanessa Johnson' – over and over would make the kids laugh. Fast forward to her time in the military, she was so funny that people in her network and those she crossed paths with were always drawn to her humor. Keitha began to declare that she was going to be a comedian. One of her friends, Mary Ellen Gross, helped her take the plunge, by actually booking her a comedy gig. The performance lit Keitha up! She was on assignment in Germany at the time. From that point, Keitha began to pursue work as a comedian. Her last military assignment before retirement was at the Pentagon which brought her to Northern Virginia.

Keitha found a new church home at Antioch Baptist Church in Fairfax Station, Virginia. Keitha decided to set up a meeting with her new pastor. It was fortuitous, as he inquired about what she planned to do after retirement. When she indicated she wanted to do comedy, he asked if she was familiar with Christian comedy. Keitha was not familiar with Christian comedy. Her pastor gave her a tape to watch of a Christian comedian performing. Seeds were planted.

One day at home, Keitha remembers hearing a clear voice telling her that it was not just comedy, but Christian comedy specifically, that the Lord wanted her to do. Keitha's manager advised her that Christian comedy would box her in. On the contrary, Keitha knew she was going to be doing comedy for God and there was no limit with Him. As a Christian Comedian, Keitha has been booked to perform throughout the United States. Her comedy highlights thus far have been as the opening comedy act at a concert by CeCe Winans and at a convention Gospel Fest featuring Richard Smallwood.

Christian Comedy was not the only door that God opened for Keitha after her military retirement. Keitha knew she didn't want to pursue civil service or anything military or government related, but she wanted to find a setting to use her array of skills and abilities. Her church called one day and asked if she would be willing to volunteer to help with some administrative work. Keitha agreed and jumped in to assist, finding the assignment easy. A paid administrative position came open within a few months after Keitha became a volunteer and she was hired. Within six months of Keitha becoming a paid employee at her church, she was promoted to be the Director of Operations! Her diverse background and experience in the Army prepared her well for the broad range of coordination and collaboration required to successfully run church operations.

Wow, Keitha vaulted forward beautifully after her military career! But that does not mean it was completely smooth sailing in her life from that point forward. Keitha experienced another major trial in the fall of 2014, when she was diagnosed with breast cancer. She traveled a long and arduous journey through chemotherapy. She believed in her heart that God was going to heal her and see to her being cancer-free. She relied completely on the Lord and lived the faith she had always spoken about. Keitha learned that her timetable and God's timetable were not the same. So much so that during her healing phase, the cancer returned in 2016, this time as stage four cancer. This time Keitha had to battle through regiments of radiation and chemotherapy, but God saw her through again! Sometimes Keitha had to face delays or setbacks and sometimes things accelerated during her treatments. She accepted that she had to put her timetable for healing on the shelf and to surrender to God's timing for her healing.

Keitha's story clearly indicates she had a great foundation of faith to hold onto when she faced major challenges in her life. What would she say to someone who does not know Christ, or someone who does not know how to develop their faith or a relationship with Christ? Keitha responded; "Just begin where you are. None of us are perfect. He accepts us the way that we are. We can't fix up to get ourselves ready for Christ. We have to say, here I am Lord, help me. Don't worry about what people are doing - not even your family. You can begin with a simple prayer such as, Lord thank you for today, or Lord, I want to change, I want to be in your family. God, I want you to walk with me. As you talk to God, He will help you to build your relationship with Him."

Looking back, Keitha acknowledged that at the time she was not selected for the promotion she wanted, it was a trial to think of that door closing. She had to lean on God and trust that He had something else for her to do. And as it turned out, the door that closed allowed her to see and pursue possibilities from God that she would not have considered. Keitha got to pursue a career as a Christian Comedian, who enlightens and encourages audiences, and to serve God's people as the Director of Ministry Services at her home church. Indeed, new doors opened! Keitha V. Johnson sees how God has blessed her abundantly as she is serving in the best Army anyone can serve in - and that is God's Army!! And she is further blessed by bringing humor and laughter to people along the way. Praise God from whom all blessings flow!!

REFLECTIONS FOR YOU:

1. On a personal level, how did Keitha's story speak to you?

2. In what area of your life have you become too comfortable?

3. Is there any place in your life that you are staring at a closed door instead of moving forward?

REACHING YOUR TRUE POTENTIAL – ANTHONY 'TONY' STAMILIO

The heart of man plans his way, but the Lord establishes his steps.
(Proverbs 16:9)

Have you ever had periods in your life that flew by? Weeks, months or even years went by that you cannot account for what you were focused on? Times where you look back and know, you were on auto pilot in your life? You may be there now, with the days of your life drifting by. What might be different in your life if you become very intentional about how you spend your days? How much more of your potential could you tap into?

Executive Coach and Consultant, Anthony 'Tony' Stamilio talked about living to our true potential, dealing with the fear of failure, and his own personal experiences and strategies which may provide you with some thought-provoking insights, professionally and personally.

Tony grew up in Corning New York, a second-generation Italian American. His grandparents on both sides immigrated to the United States in the early part of the 20th century. His parents were people of principle and modest means. His mom and dad instilled in him from their example that it's all about family and, you can do lots of things if you just put your mind to it and try. Their example gave him the core values of family, faith, trying your best and having fun.

Like most kids in his neighborhood, Tony enjoyed playing sports, and he was a pretty smart kid. His parents never questioned his actual grades, but whether he did his best. With sports, like school, after each game and practice, Tony's dad would only ask two questions, "Did you try your best?" and "Did you have a good time?" As you will see, these two questions became standard bearers for Tony and underneath those two questions he added: Did you work hard, and did you work at the right things? What a valuable strategy to have your actions in life guided by these key questions!

With this foundation, Tony seemed determined from early on to pursue his true potential and enjoy the journey along the way. He even recalled a grammar school lesson that influenced his growth and perspective. A student questioned their teacher about the difference in the students' potential and whether one with a lot of potential and another person with less potential could both reach the same level of happiness. Tony remembers his astute teacher giving the analogy of a water glass and a shot glass both being filled up. One is filled with more water, but both glasses are full. She equated reaching one's potential to when one was filled. In life, we may be the water glasses, shot glasses or somewhere in between. But if a person was doing all that he or she could to reach their potential, they would be filled and as a result experience happiness. The influence of that analogy guided Tony to try things and work as hard as he could, even if the outcome was less than successful. So, he continued to work hard.

While Tony learned that his best effort and hard work did not result in success every time, it happened often enough. He shared a few of the pivotal choices he made which illustrated how he integrated his perspectives into practice. One illustration was during his freshman year in high school. Tony thought he was going to be a star on his high school basketball team, when interestingly he was not a basketball sized person, nor was he particularly adept at basketball. On day two of try-outs, the basketball coach came to him and said, "Stamilio, let me introduce you to Coach Corcoran. He's the wrestling coach and if you work hard, you'll be able to wrestle." It turned out to be a good call to move on from basketball. Tony worked hard and wrestled in high school which was far more gratifying than sitting on the bench or merely being a cheerleader at basketball games.

Another illustration is when he was in uniform as a young major in the Army. During his first assignment at the Pentagon, a new performance appraisal system had been launched. The new system rated officers in the top half or bottom half of performers. His first rating was in the bottom half. The rating was sobering for Tony, but his mentor's advice affirmed what he already believed. "Keep working hard and try to have some fun along the way." Tony showed his resilience even after that 'bottom half' rating, and he continued on and had a successful Army career.

Something else that Tony observed also contributed significantly to reaching his true potential. The more he learned about himself and the more he understood his unique combination of strengths, passions and gifts as well as his shortfalls, the easier it was for him to take advantage of them and be successful. He became aware that oftentimes, it was not about the technical skills, but instead about the people skills. It was what you had inside that you were willing to share and to put forth in terms of effort that made the difference. In essence, Tony spoke to the fact that we can bring our whole selves forward, not just our career training and education, but our life experience, values, innate strengths and abilities on our journey to reaching our true potential.

As an executive coach and consultant, Tony helps leaders and organizations to see possibility through first growing their awareness of their current circumstances. Then from there, to become deliberate with planning steps to move forward in a positive direction. He helps leaders see the vital importance of understanding themselves and their people. This brought Tony to his observations regarding leaders and risk or fear of failure. He spoke about this pertinent challenge from his work with clients as well as his own personal and professional experience. He sees fear of failure as a huge inhibition, an albatross around the neck of a person. He has even seen among very successful executives, a crisis of confidence, being inhibited by their own sense of doubt about their abilities. For people who desire to do more and be more, the fear of failure has to be overcome. Overcoming the fear of failure necessitates just trying, the ability to take a small positive step, which will lead to other positive steps.

In Tony's own experience with fear of failure, whenever he chose to ignore the fear and give things a try, he was much more able to be successful. For Tony, when there was some risk or potential that things might not work out for him, he invested a little more of himself into the effort because he wanted to offset the risk and inhibition associated with the endeavor. This approach synced with Tony's philosophy that he adopted early on: work very hard and have some fun!

In a heartwarming story Tony described one of the first times that he really overcame a fear of failure and threw caution to the wind. It was on a first date and he declared to his date that they were going to get married. How did that come up in a first date conversation? Somehow it did and Tony told her that the two of them would be married. And what happened? His date apparently agreed because at the time of this interview, they had been married for 44 happy years! Tony recognized it as the best decision he'd ever made.

On the professional side, Tony opted to make decisions about his career path based upon what he thought was either the right thing to do or because he thought it would be more fun regardless of his apprehension and of what the organization told him he 'should' be doing. What, in Tony's view is essential for individuals and organizations to pursue their true potential? Tony responded, "Every individual, be it in an organization or daily life, has dreams, has potential and has an obligation to themselves to try and do all that they can to realize those dreams and to try to fill that glass to the fullest. First, I believe is an introspective look at what I really want to become. Second, what is the art of the possible, and third, what is one thing that I can do to start down that path? It takes some thinking, it takes some believing in yourself, and then it takes the courage to take just one step."

It is no coincidence that the "tag line" for Tony's company, *First Step Coaching & Consulting,* is "The Journey to Positive Change Starts with the First Step." Tony also reminded that your true potential has multiple dimensions, by stating; "You can assess: how am I doing professionally, spiritually, in my relationships, financially, physically, and recreationally?" Tony asserted that we may not be the best in all dimensions or we may not be the best in any, but we can be as good as we can be. And remember, sometimes the goals we set for ourselves or what we see as our potential is too limited but trusting God can bring us to a place of fulfilment that we could not have thought possible.

Along Tony's journey, has he faced unexpected challenges, detours and obstacles? Yes. Has he had to adjust his vision or plans due to unforeseen circumstances? Absolutely.

Nonetheless, Tony lives what he coaches. And as he described, learning his unique combination of strengths, passions, gifts and his shortfalls was a significant key to his success. Tony Stamilio's glass is full because he has not wavered from taking the steps to reach his true potential. And his family, his faith, trying his best and having fun continue to be his guideposts.

REFLECTIONS FOR YOU:

1. What part of Tony's story resonated with you most?

2. How often do you consider the 'fun' component of your daily life?

3. How much does fear of failure stop you from trying to reach your true potential?

FROM CHALLENGES TO BLESSINGS – REV. DR. MARSHAL AUSBERRY

Count it all joy, my brothers, when you meet trials of various kinds, for you know that the testing of your faith produces steadfastness. (James 1:2-3)

Often when we examine what our lives have entailed, particularly the trials and very challenging times, we might say our lives are not what we intended to create for ourselves. In the midst of a major challenge, we may not see it, but sometimes there are unforeseen blessings that come through afterwards. In fact, when we are walking in those subsequent blessings, some onlookers may imagine our journey has been almost free of challenges.

Reverend Doctor Marshal Ausberry's response to the notion that some might witness his flourishing today as a symbol of having a challenge-free road in life was this; "People see your glory, but don't know your story. And they don't know the struggles or process you had to go through during the late nights of restlessness or just wondering if this thing will work out or not work out." Rev. Ausberry is the Senior Pastor of Antioch Baptist Church in Fairfax Station, Virginia. H gave two poignant illustrations of major trials in his life, and how blessings ultimately followed the challenges.

One of the most challenging situations for Rev. Ausberry and his wife, Robyn was when their second child, Rian was born. She was born with severe developmental disabilities. It was crushing for them. Rian's special needs and what her care entailed were not in the script they had for their lives. Early on, Rev. Ausberry's biggest concern was for Robyn, not so much for himself. She joined a support group for mothers of special needs children. However, the initial group was not so helpful. Rev. Ausberry observed that Robyn seemed worse when she returned home from the group than she was before she left home.

How did the Ausberrys cope with and manage the reality of their daughter's special needs? They accepted God's plan for their lives. What got them through and continues to get them through is their faith in the Lord, trusting God that while it did not make sense to them, they knew that it was within His will. Robyn soon found another support group to join, this time a Christian based group. This group made a real difference; her spirits were lifted and it was obvious when she came home that Robyn was being blessed and that her perspective was enriched by this support group. The Ausberrys learned from the experience that it makes a difference to get with the right group for support when you're going through major challenges.

Robyn's second support group used a book by Robert S. McGee, *Search For Significance* as a key resource. The book explores the common issues people go through in life. It points out ways to cope with life issues and not to believe the lies of Satan. It showed the value of believing what God says about us, that we are truly wonderfully, marvelously made and that God loves us one hundred percent. It helped the Ausberrys to see it was not about their performance, but that God loves us and in turn we are to be honoring to Him. That lesson and insight really helped to turn their household around. Their prayer became "help us to be faithful parents and to love Rian and accept your will for our lives." Rev. Ausberry particularly relied on the scripture Proverbs 3:5-6 which says, *Trust in the Lord with all of your heart and lean not to your own understanding. Acknowledge Him in all your ways and He will make your paths straight.* His practical analogy of how they trusted God was like stretching out on a bed believing that bed is going to hold you every night at bedtime. Likewise, he believed when they stretched out on God, that God would sustain them and hold them up.

Career-wise at this point, Rev. Ausberry was enjoying the corporate world and his job. Things were going well and he was climbing the corporate ladder. While he had always relied upon God, he had never given his total life to God. He described it this way, "If my life were like a pie, God had seven of the eight slices of that pie." The eighth slice was his corporate career. Although Rev. Ausberry didn't speak about it this way, he shared that inside his attitude was 'God, I've got this. I don't need you in this part of my life.' During this time, as Rev. Ausberry's career was going very well and the family continued making positive adjustments with Rian, it was also a period of wrestling with God about his call into ministry.

As Rian began to grow older, Rev. Ausberry saw godliness in her. It helped him re-evaluate what was really important in his life, and he realized it was not all about the big bucks corporate career, but ultimately yielding himself to serve God. What he saw as he watched Rian grow helped him yield his will to

God's Will. In essence, Rev. Ausberry realized God used Rian to get his full attention.

Nonetheless, Rev. Ausberry did not surrender the eighth slice of his life pie immediately. In fact, it was not until after God allowed a major challenge to shake the career slice of his world, that Rev. Ausberry fully surrendered to God's call.

He felt well trained and equipped through college for the career he wanted. Rev. Ausberry had worked hard and at the time was the assistant comptroller in a company in southern VA. He even fulfilled some of the comptroller's responsibilities. He liked the comptroller job and could envision himself in that job. Eventually, the comptroller job at the company came open. Rev. Ausberry applied and interviewed for the job thinking confidently that he would land the job given that he had already fulfilled most of those responsibilities, and especially with his Master's degree in Accounting and a Certified Professional Accountant (CPA) designation. He thought he was a shoo-in for this dream job which he saw himself retiring from.

When the CEO met with him about the position, he told Rev. Ausberry that he did a great job, but it was not his time. What?? Rev. Ausberry was stunned by the CEO's decision because he thought it was the ideal job for him, with his name all over it. His disappointment was so deep that he stayed in his bathrobe for about a week. He had never been given the response 'it's not your time.' He had always been taught to work hard, do his job and equip himself and the door of opportunity would be open.

But the reality was clear: that was not always the case. The shut door caused him to begin looking for opportunities elsewhere, although that company had promised him that the next promotion would be his. But Rev. Ausberry did not want to do business that way. He moved on to another job, and moved again, feeling a bit like he was the little silver ball inside a pinball machine.

In the midst of the difficulty of accepting that he did not get his desired position, and his seeking suitable work elsewhere, he could not understand why God shut the door to his dream job. But Rev. Ausberry came to realize that when we go through trials and come out on the other side, we can look back and see that the challenges were not meant to destroy us, but to get us to where God wants us to be. And what unforeseen blessings awaited Rev. Ausberry and his family!

After his disappointment of not getting the comptroller job, Rev. Ausberry was led to take an opportunity in Northern Virginia. And from that job, he was promoted to his ultimate goal to be a Vice President! But from the day he walked into his new VP job, it was emotionally cold and empty. He felt God telling him, "I've got something else for you to do." About a year later he surrendered and said, "OK God I'll do what you want me to do, I'll be your minister." When he finally surrendered his corporate career to God, that was when God really took over! In retrospect, Rev. Ausberry recognized that it was God shutting doors on certain jobs, and God opening up the doors in Northern Virginia, and then moving him into ministry.

Once the Ausberrys got settled in Northern Virginia, they visited and eventually joined Antioch Baptist Church in Fairfax

Station, VA. While serving in Antioch, the church's then Senior Pastor, Rev. John Q. Gibbs became ill and passed away suddenly. Rev. Ausberry was voted in as Pastor of Antioch in 1995 and has served as Antioch's Senior Pastor for the last 25 years. At Antioch, the Ausberrys raised their children to adulthood. Rian is now a lovely young adult woman living with her parents and the family is deeply loved by their congregation. Rev. Ausberry considers it an honor to serve at Antioch with its warm and caring congregation. What blessings came to the Ausberry family, after two very challenging seasons.

Looking back, Rev. Ausberry always valued learning. From every situation or circumstance, he wanted to learn and consider what could have been done better. He sees himself as a lifelong learner, learning from people whom God puts in his path, along with reading, studying and taking courses.

To prepare for each new year, toward November/December time frame, Rev. Ausberry prays a prayer, "Lord, am I where you want me to be, and am I doing what you want me to be doing?" He trusts God to lead his path and wants to stay where God wants him. He looks with expectancy for how God will unfold each upcoming year. His perspective is while we make plans and lay some things out that we want to do, we have to see how God will direct our paths. Our plans are not in concrete, but more like wet cement which says to God that it's all about Him and our path for the new year is in His Hands.

At the time of this discussion, Rev. Ausberry felt the Lord moved him to Antioch in order to have a broader outreach to all who will receive it. Antioch's purpose statement is *Loving*

God, Loving Others. God has burdened his heart that Antioch needs to be more inclusive, and more intentional in reaching out to others. Whether it be the Hispanic Latino community, the Asian community, the Indian American community or the Anglo community, the ministries at Antioch are relevant to everyone, because God loves everyone.

As a pastor, Rev. Ausberry hears a myriad of challenges that people are grappling with. One of his common observations is that most people don't have anyone to talk with. Most people won't open up to someone for fear of being judged. But everyone needs a confidant that they trust, someone who will love them and be straight with them. God didn't call us to walk the journey by ourselves. We all need wise counsel, especially in the midst of a storm. Rev. Ausberry closed our conversation this way, "When we are not talking to someone, we tend to think our situation is hopeless. That's when the enemy tries to attack. Never lose hope, no matter how dark the moment is, how still the night, how desperate the situation might be - never, never, ever lose hope."

As Rev. Dr. Marshal Ausberry's own story so clearly depicted, what was a time of great challenge, his closing the door on a career position he longed for, was a necessary step for him to have doors open to the unforeseen blessings of full-time ministry. Remember, blessings can come after our greatest challenges!!

REFLECTIONS FOR YOU:

1. What part of Rev. Ausberry's story is most enlightening to you?

2. Have you ever had great anticipation of something happening in your life that did not happen? How did you deal with the disappointment?

3. When you are in a season of challenges, do you try to manage it alone or do you have someone that you can trust and confide in?

DWELL IN POSSIBILITY – TONI TOWNES-WHITLEY

Jesus replied, "What is impossible with man is possible with God." (Luke 18:27)

What do you think of when you hear the expression, "Perspective is everything?" How true is that for you? When we are walking down a street, we will look at the area around us from one perspective, but if we drive down the same street in a luxury car, we can have an altogether different perspective. It's so easy to define and scope a situation or challenge from our own particular perspective, that is, until something or someone helps us see things from a different point of view.

During Women's History Month a few years ago, a woman who is a trailblazer in her personal and professional life, sat down for a conversation about her journey, challenges, perspectives and possibilities from where she sits today. We'll hear the value of perspective in the life of a woman who has lived in different parts of the world, been a Peace Corps volunteer and today serves as a senior executive in a Fortune 500 company.

Toni Townes-Whitley is a military brat, a very proud daughter of an Army veteran who retired as a three-star general after beginning his career as an enlisted soldier, serving during a time when opportunities were still quite limited for African American men in the military. Toni's mom was a school principal who had an amazing career blazing new trails, particularly in elementary education throughout Fairfax County, Virginia.

Growing up as a military daughter, with numerous

relocations over her years of school, Toni learned early that she needed to be agile. She learned that she needed to make friends quickly, adapt quickly and gain the best from their situation and setting. Also, quite frankly Toni learned to look forward, and not get too nestled in at any one place or it would be much too difficult to leave when the time came. Toni's early years taught her valuable lessons and adaptability that she's been able to continue to leverage well across the adult seasons of her life.

Our core values as adults are often shaped in large part by how we grow up. Toni described her core values as built upon fundamental pre-programming by her parents, extended family and church family. Her values include living out bible verses such as Luke 12:48, *...to whom much is given, much will be required* and Philippians 4:13, *"I can do all things through Christ who strengthens me."* Toni knows how her steps could be ordered and chiefly, she knows her source of joy, which does not come from her job, or society or some form of recognition. She aptly stated, "What I do is not who I am." Instead, she knows that her source of joy comes back to her faith. Because of the pre-programming, Toni defaults to walking out her core values. She shows up freely, authentically and whole, no matter what circumstance or difficulty she may be facing.

Toni went on to describe her attention and care around giving employees feedback. She believes it should be precise, clear and transparent - delivered not to harm, but to heal and help people move forward. She gives balanced feedback. When giving positive feedback to women in the workplace, she encourages those who receive feedback to take the positives as a directional point in which to proceed further. However, she finds sometimes that women in the workplace may feast on negative or developmental feedback while quickly moving past positive feedback. Toni advises that women pay attention to what they focus on. If they can begin to see their strengths and what's working well, celebrate their achievements, and dwell in possibility, they will feel more confident in their capabilities to handle new challenges, as they are given greater responsibilities and keep moving forward.

As an executive at a Fortune 500 company, Toni finds she leverages all of her personal and professional experience over her past career to her current position, which she calls a 'full body workout.' She draws upon everything...from her past travel as a military brat, and life on the equator as a Peace Corps volunteer which taught her cross-cultural values, to her athletic background which taught her to be able to meet the physical and mental strength demands required for the extensive travel in her work today. Further, she draws upon her academic training as an economist prior to entering the technology industry, which differentiated her with modeling and analytics competencies so critical to our evolution into a digital economy. Toni uses being a mother, wife, daughter, sister, and every talent and experience at her disposal in her current role to achieve the mission.

Toni is experiencing tremendous success and impact. She dwells in possibility today and influences countless women to do the same. Yet she too has had difficult trials to walk through and her experiences have given her perspective. A few of her examples: After graduating from Princeton's Woodrow Wilson School with a degree in economics, at 22 years of age, Toni joined the Peace Corps. She was assigned to Gabon in Central Africa, a French speaking nation. Toni had studied French and felt comfortable with the language. But she came with the arrogance of a 22-year-old...that she was going to solve all the problems of the village with her teachings. As she got into the village and began to work with some of the women in the village, they had to take a fairly long walk (about a three kilometer-round trip) to get water. Toni found that this walk was not as efficient as it could have been. With her Western thinking, she had a vision of capturing and using the rainwater that came down so heavily on the tin roofs which would prevent the women from having to walk the distance or carry the heavy pails of water back to their homes.

Toni secured money from the U.S. Embassy for what is called a Women in Development Project. They built roughly 33 water stations in a couple of villages. Unfortunately, Toni came to understand that her work had disrupted the village, and quite frankly even disrupted some of the marriages. The project had introduced some expensive tools for women to use, tools that women could even sell and have as much money as their husbands earned in a year. Further, Toni recognized after three months of building water stations, that she had created a village that almost looked like an urban city in the United States. No one left their homes. They had their water. Nobody came out. The festivals in the middle of the village stopped. No one walked or even really talked as much during the day.

From her view, Toni was solving a problem; the walk was too long, the water was too heavy to carry and she had an efficient way to address it. However, what Toni eventually understood was that the walk was not about the water. The walk was about women of many generations teaching each other what it was to be a Gabonese woman. The walk was seminal, like a rite of passage for young girls. It was a sacred, special time. While Toni worried about how much time it took, the time was a gift that the women were giving to each other.

Toni had to go back and repair some relationships and extend apologizes throughout the village. Fortunately, the water stations still remain in Gabon, over 30 years later. They are used by older women or when babies are sick. The women resumed walking to the water because the walk meant something. Toni's perspective broadened considerably from the experience. When she consults around the world, she's aware that particularly around technology, that all have a bias or a blind spot. Toni recognized that when she and her team humble themselves, they can learn why it is that things seem inefficient but can hold an underlying purpose or a different value in non-Western cultures. Ultimately, the experience helped Toni to not only be aware of her own biases, but also biases around her so that she can really understand a situation and think before making a recommendation.

Another very tough trial Toni described grew her perspective immeasurably. It occurred when she worked for a system integrator in the D.C. market, when an inappropriate and incorrect assumption was made that her 30-year friendship with the then first lady of the United States had led to her company landing a major government contract. A combination of incorrect information and inflammatory language went viral on social media to the point that reporters tried to contact Toni's children, plus her receiving threats and really hateful messages. The whole thing caught Toni totally off guard. Even when presented with the actual facts of the matter, that the contract had nothing to do with Toni, it was of no interest to some who stuck with and spread their erroneous conclusions.

The entire incident was so ridiculous that she assumed it would quickly dissipate, but it did not. It was a really difficult time for Toni as her reputation was maligned in the press. At first Toni admittedly wanted to lock herself away in her home, as she had a hard time believing what was happening. But when the accuracy and professionalism that she expected did not prevail, Toni fell back on her pre-programming; her core values. Friends and family stood around her as her reputation and integrity spoke for her. She went back to the bible verse that she'd held all of her life; ...*to whom much is given, much will be required.* In this case she accepted that what was required of her was to take some hits, to stand and not to fear wrong perceptions, nor to be ashamed of the truth. Toni also got quiet and prayed. She heard from the Lord when it was time to take a stand on the truth, and that He would bring her the opportunity. Thus, Toni did the opposite of shutting herself in at home. Within a month of the original story launching, she accepted an invitation to attend an event by one of the organizations she supports. There, in front of a packed house, she was invited to share her story.

Toni's remarks struck a chord with the audience. Afterwards, some of them mentioned going through something similar, many thanked her for standing up, for her reputation, and for not overly defending herself or answering insulting questions. Toni found redemption in that opportunity (which came to her) to share her story in a public venue. Her faith proved to be the underpinning not only of who she is but how she operates. What a weighty experience of gaining perspective! Toni showed that even in the midst of significant challenges through work, she would continue to stand and continue to seek ways to bring glory to God!

The two examples Toni shared illustrates how valuable and instructive gaining perspective can be, no matter what you're facing. In fact, Toni finds the topic of perspective woven into the most common pieces of advice that she gives to others experiencing trials, whether professionally or personally. Toni's key points:

1. Pull back and look at the situation from a different angle. Any situation or challenge looks a certain way head on. But once you seek a new vantage point, you may gain new insights into the challenge. Sometimes the answers for work come from home. And the answers for a home challenge may come at work.

2. Take a break from focusing on the challenge. Give your mind a rest. It's often when you are thinking about

or focused on something other than the challenge at hand that you'll gain insight and perspective on your challenge.

3. Separate your ego from the challenge. Can we be taking a situation too personally because our egos are involved? What can we learn from the challenge if we examine it objectively?

4. Consider the worst-case scenario. When you look at your challenge, what is the worst thing that could happen? Now for perspective, think of what could be the worst-case scenarios for a fireman, a pilot or a trauma surgeon.

5. Ask yourself, what do I need to see in a broader way so that I can engage better?

Toni's success with perspective also allows her to be more intentional about how she uses her energy and time. And how does Toni dwell in possibility and continue to grow as a leader? She creates the space to do so. It's essential for Toni to have a time of refreshing and knowing what gives her energy. She gets a lot of energy from her family, enjoying her husband, kids, grandkids, parents and siblings. Hanging out with friends and coming together to enjoy them all together with lots of food is refreshing for her. Toni also finds that writing is very rejuvenating. She has four or five writing projects going at any time, including her work on a screenplay! Travel and being near physical beauty, whether near the water or the mountains, and just getting off the beaten path to enjoy unique experiences are stimulating. Being with family and friends, exposing herself to variety and surprise experiences fuels Toni and gives her the space to dwell in possibility.

What comes to mind for Toni regarding a legacy or one day a description of the life she led? Toni ultimately summed up how she wants to be remembered this way. Love Fiercely ~ Live Fearlessly ~ Learn Forgiveness. What a model of the qualities and character that uplift the world!! Thank you, Toni Townes-Whitley, for your impact of living a fiercely loving, fearless and forgiving life!!

REFLECTIONS FOR YOU:

1. What is your most significant personal takeaway from Toni's story?

2. When has your perspective on a situation hindered your well-being?

3. Where in your life do you want to see new possibility?

4. What words do you want to describe the life you have led?

CHAPTER THREE

OVERCOMING HEALTH CHALLENGES

SEEING CHALLENGES AS PREPARATION – DR. JOE LEE

For we are His workmanship, created in Christ Jesus for good works, which God prepared beforehand so that we would walk in them. (Ephesians 2:10)

What Have Your Challenges Prepared You to Do? This may sound like a strange question. Because when trials or challenges are in your face, you may be more likely to ask yourself –why is this happening to me? Or, how will I ever get through this? But looking back, what have you learned when facing some of your biggest challenges in your life? Did you learn to not give up? To believe in yourself? What did you learn about going further and achieving more than you thought you could? Your lessons may be any combination of these. If not, after you hear Dr. Joe Lee's story, you may answer the question, what have your challenges prepared you to do differently? Sometimes it is the very questions that we ask ourselves that make all the difference in how we manage any challenging situation.

Dr. Joe A Lee, a graduate of Talladega College, served as Dean of Students while I was a student there in the late 1970s. After he graduated from Talladega College, he returned to his hometown, committed to educating the youth at his former high school, Southern Normal School in Brewton, Alabama. There he taught biology, chemistry and physics. Afterwards he went back to his Alma Mater, Talladega College, where over the years he served in numerous capacities which culminated in 1994 with him being named Vice President for Academic

Affairs and Provost. Between 1995 and 2008, Dr. Lee served as President of both Tugaloo College in Mississippi and Alabama State University in Alabama. Dr. Lee balanced Tugaloo's multimillion-dollar budget while he oversaw major upgrades to the 132-year-old campus. From there, he became president of Alabama State University, and under his leadership the school was approved to offer its first of several doctoral programs and witnessed an extensive multimillion-dollar building program.

Dr. Lee has vast experience with board appointments at the national, regional and local levels with civic, educational and community service organizations such as chairing the advisory board of the National Institute of Minority Health, Family, and Community Violence Prevention Program, serving on the National Board for the United Negro College Fund, and a Director for the United Way Board in Jackson Mississippi. In Mississippi he also served on the Board of Directors of the Jackson area American Red Cross and as a mentor for Powell Middle School and Poindexter Elementary School. While President at Alabama State, Dr. Lee served on the Board of Directors for the Metro YMCA, the Montgomery Area Chamber of Commerce Committee of 100 and there he was also appointed by the Secretary of Defense to the Air Force's Air University Board of Visitors. His dynamic leadership has led to Dr. Lee receiving numerous citations and awards such as the UNCF's Individual Excellence Award, an annual scholarship named in his honor by the Greater Talladega area Chamber of Commerce. Although Dr. Lee retired in 2010, he came out of retirement to serve as Provost and Vice President for Academic

Affairs at Cambridge College in Cambridge, Massachusetts until January 2012 when he resumed retirement and moved to Florida where he enjoys time with his family.

Do you notice the loads of accomplishments? Do you observe Dr. Lee's commitment to serving others? Can you sense his dedicated leadership and intention to make a positive impact for others? I did too, and it inspired me to want to understand what his life had been like on the way to a season of so much achievement, influence and service. I wondered what kind of challenges he might have faced in his journey that knitted together a calling to make such sacrifice and such a difference, along with a tangible desire to lift others up? His story answered those questions.

Dr. Lee grew up in South Alabama, poor. His parents raised nine children, six boys and three girls. At six years old, Dr. Lee contracted polio. One day at school, he got scratched and didn't bleed, only clear fluid came out. He was rushed to the hospital and spent the next eleven months in the hospital with polio. He weighed only 35 pounds. He knew there were a lot of people who prayed for him and stayed with him to make sure he had the best that he could get as a young black boy growing up in Brewton, Alabama. Dr. Lee noted that the most common theme over his lifetime was not to let people or your condition dictate your station in life. You can only let either other people or your station -or both- put you in a position of saying "I will never be able to accomplish anything." He remembers wanting to do things and hearing people in the community say that he would never do things because his family didn't have the resources.

But he found from a young age that aside from the naysayers, there was someone at every juncture in his life that provided an opportunity. He determined early in his life to take advantage of the opportunities.

Dr. Lee recalled that the thread took root as early as during his battle with polio. He lay semi-conscious in a hospital room with his parents also in the room, when he heard the doctor tell his parents that he would not survive the night and suggested to them that they call the family together and make a decision. The doctor told the Lees that there was no way they would be able to afford the hospital bill. Therefore, the doctor had a proposal for Dr. Lee's parents. He stated there was a university that wanted to use their son's body to study the effects of polio and the donation of his remains to the university would offset his hospital expenses. Let that proposal to the parents of a six-year-old sink in for a moment. Dr. Lee's father was a laborer who did any type of work he could find to keep his family going. His mother was a domestic who kept the children of others during their workday. Instead of immediately accepting the doctor's prognosis and agreeing to donate their son's body to science, they took a most courageous and notable step. Albeit they were a poor family, they made all of their decisions as a family at the dinner table. His parents shared with his siblings what the doctor had explained and what he offered.

The Lee family voted no, that they would not give up on their son and sibling. They figured if it was God's desire, they would find a way to pay the hospital bill. Despite the doctor's grim prognosis, Dr. Lee lived!! His parents were determined to help their son regain full health. A nurse took special interest in him. She, the doctor and others in the community even helped his family pay the hospital bill. Once he was home when his braces were removed, his mother massaged his legs, performing a type of divinely-led physical therapy that helped him to strengthen his muscles and eventually regain use of his legs. Not only that, but although Dr. Lee suffered some effects from his bout with polio up to about age 10, by age 16, he was able to fulfill his desire to play high school football!

Dr. Lee still had to deal with the continual drumbeat of hearing that he wouldn't make it. But as he stated earlier, there were always angels that allowed him to keep moving forward. He noted several examples. When he got out of the hospital, he was up to date because certain teachers even brought his schoolwork to the hospital and a nurse ensured he did his homework. Nonetheless, when Dr. Lee graduated from high school, the prospects seemed dim for what he could do next from Brewton, Alabama. But a guidance counselor (angel) proclaimed that he was going to do something and not just stay at home. Not long before the new college year began, an alumni of Talladega College (Mae Graham Young) called the school and advocated for scholarships for Dr. Lee and some other students. At Talladega, a biology professor wanted him to apply for an opportunity to become a park ranger in the Great Smoky Mountains National Park. With that endorsement, he and two other students applied and indeed in 1967 became the first black park rangers for that National Park!

One certainty in Dr. Lee's life was that God was in his past, present and future. Over his entire life, God's grace placed the angels on his shoulders. What had Dr. Lee's challenges prepared him to do? It not only prepared him, but it also challenged him to give back, it helped him to say thank you to his mom and dad and to his wife's parents for having faith in what he could do. And to have gratitude to all of the angels along his journey (e.g., Claire Woodson, Lew Paugman, Mae Graham Young, Tia Andrews, Nurse Lyston Stallworth, Robert Lowe, and the list goes on and on) who saw something in him and nurtured him. Dr. Lee's challenges also prepared him to have faith in his students, even for those who required disciplinary actions or 'tough love.' He could see something in them maybe beyond what they could see, just like someone had seen the potential in him.

Over his entire career, Dr. Lee's quest or need has been to give back and show his appreciation for all of those who came to his rescue that he can't pay back, so he pays it forward. Margie, his wife, attests that their desire in life was never to be rich. They desired to be comfortable, but every time they got something, they wanted to give something.

Over Dr. Lee's life, two things kept him mindful of the importance of giving back: first, his battle with polio and the amazing outcome of living through that most difficult challenge against the odds, and second, was overcoming the voices of naysayers saying, "you won't make it."

Dr. Lee avidly reflected, "once you have been in a position where all of the resources that your family has are exhausted and yet you still see opportunity knocking at your door, you know that it has to be something greater than your immediate circumstances that gave you that opportunity. To have had the opportunity to serve on boards and committees that have affected folks all over the world, and to lead some of the greatest institutions in the country, that's something that doesn't happen every day. It had to be by the grace of God. I then have to make available opportunity for others to experience those same things."

Today Dr. Lee ruminates on a life of service, giving back and creating opportunities for others as someone did for him. He has a mountain of experiences where his life has touched and enriched others through his leadership, civic and community service roles. He has had the opportunities to dine with kings and queens and presidents and to travel throughout the U.S. and the world. And all because somebody saw something in him a long time ago and he took advantage of the opportunities presented to him. Dr. Lee's challenges prepared him for a destiny of serving to enrich the lives of others. As a result, there are people across the globe who share a debt that hopefully they too are paying forward. It's a debt not only to him, but to the myriad of individuals (angels) along his journey who have impacted the world through their support of and faith in Dr. Joe Lee.

UPDATE: Five years ago, Dr. Lee once again faced a grim prognosis from doctors. This time he and his family were told that due to cancer, he had only three to six months to live and that he needed to get his affairs in order. While the doctor's prognosis prompted tears from family members, Joe reflected on the great life he has lived. That was five years ago. Today his amazed oncology team tells him, "Whatever you're doing, keep doing it!" He recognizes why he is still here and tells his team, it is because of Jesus. So, what is Dr. Lee doing while he's still here? Still inspiring and still serving...helping to find scholarships for students, donating computers (even his own), and working to get internet connectivity into homes that he learns of without those resources. These are just a couple of the ways that Dr. Joe Lee is still paying it forward. Let us collectively pray for his continued strength and for God to shower him with His Amazing Grace!!!

REFLECTIONS FOR YOU:

1. In what ways can you personally relate to Dr. Joe Lee's story?

2. Considering a major challenge you have faced, how was it ultimately helpful in the long run? What did it prepare you to do?

3. How do you respond when naysayers say you can't do something?

LIFE CHANGING HEALTH CHALLENGES – MARK AND BRENDA MOORE

No temptation has overtaken you except what is common to mankind. And God is faithful; he will not let you be tempted beyond what you can bear. But when you are tempted, he will also provide a way out so that you can endure it. (1 Corinthians 10:13)

Sometimes in our lives, things are moving along smoothly, we have a happy, loving family life and a rewarding career. Our children are doing well academically, professionally and socially. Our finances are solid. We may be very busy, but we get to do things we enjoy as well. We are thriving and feeling blessed and then…an unimaginable crisis brings everything to a sudden screeching halt. This is exactly what happened in the lives of Mark and Brenda Moore.

Mark and Brenda who were high school sweethearts had been married for over 32 years at the time. They grew up in Queens, New York with humble beginnings. Over their many years together, a few common themes carried them: 1) Be humble and know that you can learn something from everybody, so really pay attention and be available. 2) Practice the golden rule - do unto others as you would have them do unto you. 3) Wrap everything in prayer. And 4) Be resilient in life. Sometimes you're knocked down, and you have to be able to get back up and keep moving forward.

Mark, a self-described Type A personality, served as Chief Operating Officer, Executive VP and Partner/Owner of Segovia Inc., a company that provided global IT services to the Department of Defense. With 20+ years of operational and financial experience, he helped to raise over $2 billion in public and private capital for his company. Earlier, as Chief Financial Officer of USA Communications, Mark completed their IPO raising $225 million dollars in public equity and a billion dollars in total capital. During these same years, Brenda was also thriving in her career as a registered nurse in obstetrics and pediatrics, and in human resources as a nurse recruiter. Mark, Brenda and their two children, Jenee and Markus, were living happily, successfully, and healthfully up until January of 2007.

Mark began to experience severe migraine headaches. The migraines were so severe that after the second one, Mark went to a neurologist to ascertain what was going on. After a litany of tests over four months, the cause of the debilitating headaches was still undetermined. It was a whole year later, that a specialty neurology team discovered that he had a congenital blood deficiency which made his blood clot – causing an imbalance.

But the time in question, the Thursday before Mother's Day of 2007, Mark played two hours of full court basketball, which he loved. Two days later, on a very hot Saturday afternoon, while he coached his son's baseball game, Mark started to have symptoms indicating that something was wrong. Nonetheless, after the game, he drove to the store with his son as planned to get Brenda a Mother's Day card. However, Mark had to be rushed to the hospital, where they diagnosed he had suffered a stroke. Only two days after Mark was admitted to the hospital, he suffered a second stroke, after which he was put into a medically induced coma for six weeks. Before either of these strokes, Mark, at 46 years old, had been in excellent physical health.

What went through the mind of a man at the top of his game physically, personally and professionally when he heard that in a matter of a couple of days, he had suffered back-to-back strokes? When Brenda was able to tell Mark what had happened, he was devastated. At 46, with his own company, he couldn't believe he had been in the hospital for six weeks, nor could he imagine that he had suffered not one, but two strokes. Imagine being told that your life had hung in the balance, and recovery was just getting started. Somehow, Mark began to reflect upon the good life he had led up to that point.

As Mark contemplated his fate, he seemed to quickly shift to accepting whatever lay ahead for him. He remembered something that his mother told him back in New York, when he was 11 or 12 years old, some 35 years earlier. She told him and her other seven children, that God only gives you what He knows you can handle, a reference found in scripture in 1 Corinthians 10:13. Those words from his mother that Mark remembered that night had not crossed his mind for 35 years! Those words moved Mark out of a feeling of devastation to an attitude that if God had given this to him, God knew he could handle it. Mark decided to do what he could do, and leave the rest to God.

This life changing health challenge began a journey of surrendering. Mark could not walk and he had lost the use of his left side. And upon his release from the six-week hospitalization, he would need three months of intensive rehabilitation. It was difficult because Mark, like many in the corporate sector, liked to be in control. And if Mark was to complete rehabilitation and fully recover, he realized he was no longer in control. He would be tested and reminded to surrender over and over again through each phase of the arduous journey to recovery.

For Brenda, even though he had suffered the headaches earlier in the year, when these two strokes came, they were a complete shock. She first thought Mark would be going home within a matter of days. But he started to have other symptoms. Brenda noticed things were changing and decided to quickly get help. The diagnostics revealed Mark had intracranial bleeding, causing a lot of pressure on his brain which required him to have immediate surgery.

A doctor who was not assigned to Mark, happened to see the results of his scans. She came to Brenda, explained she was taking over the case and brought the forms for Brenda to sign for the emergency surgery. The doctor told Brenda she was not sure what the outcome would be but they would do everything they could. Her next words were the most devastating for Brenda to hear. The doctor said Mark was in 'grave condition.' As a nurse, Brenda knew the expression 'grave condition' was rarely used in the medical profession unless it was almost hopeless.

It was a clear signal to Brenda just how bad things were. At that moment she cried out to the Lord, a blood curdling cry, as she dropped to her knees surrounded by family and friends. In that instant, she let it go. And she felt a peace that she had never experienced before, nor to that same level again since. Brenda first felt a powerlessness, but then a powerfulness immediately after that. She knew that her prayers would be answered; and whatever the Lord decided was the right thing, He would strengthen both of them. Admittedly the fear of the unknown was most difficult. However, Brenda knew they were in a good place with the right people, and God would direct their hands and their hearts.

How did the Moore family cope? Their faith in Christ was integral to coping with this life changing challenge. Up to that point in their relationship, Mark and Brenda had not prayed together regularly. But that changed. They prayed, trusted and essentially turned it over to God. Even during times when Mark was unable to speak well, during intubation and his brain resting, the Moores learned a way to communicate and pray together. They learned to integrate the word acceptance into their prayers and discussions, unsure of what the future would be. At the time their daughter was in her early 20s and their son still a teen. Faith was the center of their discussions to explain what had happened to their Dad. And whatever the outcome would be, they would be accepting whether it was what they prayed for or not.

Brenda learned to be an encourager, to stand back and observe, to listen to the health professionals and be an advocate for Mark. She found it important to be empathetic and to try and put herself in Mark's place to better understand his challenges. She was at his bedside as often as possible. She learned to accept help and support from others when they offered it and to ask for help when others did not see her needs. Mark too, noted the importance of relying on others and not trying to get through a huge health challenge alone. He came to rely heavily on his 'faith, family and friends.'

Mark remembered medical professionals discussing with him the stages and range of emotions common to a life-threatening illness, and that he could expect to experience denial, anger and fear, and that eventually acceptance and hope would come. Mark did not physically act out by throwing or breaking things, but he recalled an internal seething after Brenda told him what happened. It made no sense to him, and he recalled the tandem between anger and denial. When he was told he could not walk, or use his left limbs, his reaction was, "What are you talking about? This can't be! I was just playing basketball, of course I can walk." But the reality sank in as he sat there without being able to take a safe step on his own. Mark definitely had a lot before him on his recovery journey. And although medical professionals emphasized to him that eventually acceptance and hope would come, he preferred the terms surrender and faith. Acceptance was about surrendering. He had to continue trusting in God. And for Mark, hope was having faith.

Mark began to pray a simple prayer, "Lord, just give me the strength to deal with whatever comes my way." This was a significant change for this 'Type A' personality corporate executive, which even surprised him. He knew that the old him would have been praying for the strength to walk again, the strength to get back to work again, or to play basketball again.

But Mark did not pray for those things. His simple petition was a surrender; it was part of Mark having the faith to put his trust in God's hands, whatever happened. Before that simple invocation, the mountain of recovery looked and felt too big for him to climb. And it was. But the minute he put his trust in God and spoke that simple prayer, it had a calming effect. And with that, the mountain did not look as large. The prayer enabled Mark to focus on the things he could control, which was to work on his recovery.

For the entire six weeks of hospitalization, Brenda slept in Mark's room every night, to make sure he was okay. Then during the months of rehabilitation, Brenda drove Mark from Reston, VA to Mount Vernon Hospital in Alexandria, VA three or four days a week -- for three to four hours of therapy each time.

On day two of the rehabilitation, Mark's Type A personality resurfaced. After only one day of rehabilitation, Mark was surprised that he still was not walking. On the way home he lamented that he was not making the kind of progress that he thought he should be. Brenda pulled the car over and told him: "Tony (her pet name for him), you have no idea what the good Lord has in store for you. You don't know, maybe He allowed these strokes because He wants you to show others you can recover." Brenda's words were wise and reminded Mark that he was on a faith journey. Her reminders renewed his faith time and again.

Mark also found great encouragement and fortitude listening to gospel music during his therapy. Additionally, humor became therapeutic and Mark, Brenda and their children resumed the gaiety and fun in their lives while in recovery and rehab. It was a family mission. They did not sit down and feel sorry for themselves. They began to laugh again and have joy in their lives, even as their road and future were sometimes a bit rough or uncertain.

Over the next several months in his multi-hour rehabilitation sessions, Brenda observed as Mark learned to walk again, to tie his shoes and other simple actions that he had once taken for granted. It was a physical, mental, and spiritual challenge. Mark did the hard work to make a full recovery from two strokes!

After he began walking again in September 2007, a couple of months later, in November 2007 he got on a treadmill. But even more incredibly, in May 2008, one year after his strokes, Mark registered for a 5K run in downtown Washington, DC! He did not know what to expect. Before the strokes, Mark had enjoyed basketball and softball, but he had never been a runner. When he arrived in DC, he closed his eyes and once again said a simple prayer, asking God to give him the courage to run the race. Mark credits the Lord for helping him complete the 5K run. And he completed the 5K in 36 minutes, at a sub-12-minute mile pace. Phenomenal!!

At the time of our discussion, ten years had passed since the unimaginable crisis disrupted the lives of the Moores. Mark remains in excellent health and works out every other day. In 2012, they established the Mark and Brenda Moore and Family Foundation. The couple always had philanthropy on their radar, and now had the opportunity to create a way to have greater positive impact. Mark and Brenda set as their foundation's maxim: "Establishing Roots and Stretching Wings" which signifies honoring their parents for their hard work and sacrifice (Roots), and their reaching out to touch the lives of others in order to make a difference while also creating a legacy for their children as they move forward (Wings). Their organization's pillars of outreach are: health care, education, music and the arts, and Christian evangelism.

Due to their faith and trust in God, Mark, Brenda and their family were able to fully resume their happy, successful and healthy lives after living through a life changing health challenge. Today they are passionate philanthropists ensuring that they are positively giving back and helping others to be healthy, expand and grow, both locally and nationally.

UPDATE: Mark has written a book, *A Stroke of Faith*, which chronicles his entire journey and transformation due to his major health challenge. It is available at bookstores and online.

REFLECTIONS FOR YOU:

1. What was most significant to you personally from Mark and Brenda's story?

2. Have you ever faced a crisis that brought you to a sudden screeching halt?

3. What did you learn and do differently after facing such a crisis in your life?

CARING FOR YOUR MIND BODY AND SPIRIT -
FELICEA MYER-DELOATCH

Jesus declared, "Love the Lord your God with all your heart and with all your soul and with all your mind. (Matthew 22:37)

Caring for ourselves, holistically includes care of the body, mind and spirit. But in our busy lives, some might ask is one part more important to focus on than the others? Felicea Myer-DeLoatch answered that question and gave insights and numerous practical tips that can enliven our perspectives on the importance and benefits of a holistic approach to taking care of ourselves.

At the time of our conversation, Felicea was a clinical social worker providing therapy in her private practice, as well as working as a school social worker serving students with severe and multiple disabilities along with their families. So why does she view taking care of the mind, body & spirit as so important? Felecia sees it as self-care and ultimately about our well-being. It is a blend of some new practices, but also some historical practices about how to care for the temple God has given to each of us. And for her, the temple is not just the physical, the mental or the spiritual, but all three fundamental aspects of ourselves.

Felicea is often asked the question, Is one part more important to focus on than the others? She responds that it would be like saying the right arm is more important than the left arm, or our thoughts have more value than our physical strength. We need a strongly functioning mind, body and spirit for balance as they all serve a purpose and are interrelated. Look at it this way; our brain drives our thoughts, and without good nutrition (diet) the brain doesn't operate at one hundred percent. What we think determines how we feel. How we feel affects our attitude and even our perspectives in life. This leads to the ways we act and react to what occurs in our lives and environment. And our actions or reactions affect us physically and emotionally. When any one aspect of our mind, body or spirit is off kilter, we are therefore off balance, because the other aspects will be off kilter as well.

On the other hand, if we are taking good care of all three aspects of our lives, we are healthy and more able to live fulfilling lives where we are available to care for others. In fact, believers are called to be the hands and feet of Christ. We can be willing vessels of God, but we can be used to an even greater extent if we are willing *and healthy* vessels. It thus requires us to take care of all three dimensions as they are fundamental, integral aspects of our human selves.

Taking care of our mind, body and spirit involves time, and lack of time is one of the main obstacles faced in order to practice good self-care. Felicea posed some thought-provoking questions that may serve as inspiration. What if we accept the fact that God gave us our temples to use in ways that honor and glorify Him? What if we demonstrate that everything we do is for His Glory? What difference would that make in keeping a time commitment to consistently care for your mind, body and spirit if it was a way of honoring Christ?

In Felicea's life, she holds Christ as her center. Her lifestyle exemplifies how much she values the commitment of consistently taking care of her mind, body and spirit. Her balance and calm demeanor have even caused some people to express their surprise and wonder at how she is equipped to help clients who have experienced a lot of trauma, or multiple disabilities, or may have financial issues or other serious difficulties in their lives. Was Felicea's own life always so charmed that she never experienced a season of major trials, or had never been up close with difficult periods in her life? Nope.

When we peek into her early life, we see a background that prepared Felicea to help others to cope with life challenges. She grew up in the inner-city projects of Seattle, Washington with a single mom. She and her father maintained a close connection. But her part of Felicea's preparation to help others began at home. Her mom was a foster mother who adopted 11 children, 10 of them with disabilities. Felicea was the oldest child and her growing up years required a lot of work on her part, helping her mom with her many siblings.

Reflecting on those difficult growing up years, with so many responsibilities of family, school, and community, what is one of Felicea's biggest lessons? In fact, her childhood gave her a lot of strength and resilience. And notably, her younger years gave Felicea a lens through which to look at the world as there is really nothing that we cannot do. Her mother and father were definitive in the perspective that doing for others is a must. There was never a question of how much you had, but rather one of what others needed. Wow!

While we all go through challenging times, Felicea emphasized that we can build resilience into our lives and learn how to rebound faster and stronger from our challenges. Learning resilience lets us train our body, mind and spirit to respond to trials in a productive manner. We will still have human responses to challenges. Of course, we will experience disappointment, frustration, or anger sometimes. God gave us our emotions. But we get to choose to make mindful choices about our responses to issues, even during a crisis. We can choose to do all things with love and a measure of grace. When we fall down, we can choose to get up and begin again. We get to choose whether to stay stuck or to take steps to move forward. We can get help when we need it or we can try to bear all of our tough challenges on our own

One vital component Felicea shared to nourish our mind, body and spirit, is to wake up each day with gratitude. She explained, "Even in the midst of tragedies out in the world that we see in the media, as well as with the events that impact us directly, we can find something to be grateful for. We can live a life recognizing that God is in control and has a plan. He is sovereign. It feeds our spirit and eases our mind when we can walk in inner peace with the idea that we are here to serve and honor God, so how can we do so today?" What a shift in our lives we could experience by trying more gratitude! Felicea's viewpoint was clear, "When we look at our whole lives through a lens of gratefulness, our spirit no longer sees itself through a lens of helplessness, or lack, or being a victim. Instead, we get to live with joy and blessings that come to us without our looking for them."

Practices of taking care of the mind, body and spirit are good for the whole family. No age is too young or too old. Parents can teach children that they have a choice in how they react to circumstances, to be grateful, to eat healthy foods to exercise, and to rest well as often as possible. In other words, practicing good self-care is both modeling and teaching valuable life skills to our family members.

Felicea emphasized a few other practical ideas to take care of mind, body and spirit:

1. Solid, uninterrupted sleep is so essential. That is, sleep with no video screens, televisions, phones or electronic reading devices. When we read at bedtime on electronic devices, we are activating our brain and creating chemical reactions that prevent the brain from shutting down for rest. Research shows that it takes about an hour after the exposure to electronic devices for our brains to really slow down.

   Felicea noted that it is helpful to move away from electronic devices at least an hour before you go to bed. Instead, try reading a bound book, praying, practicing meditation or visualization exercises to calm your mind, body and spirit.

   After you brush your teeth or change for bed, it may be helpful to have a scent e.g., lavender or eucalyptus in a lotion or spray, or playing soft, relaxing music each night can train your brain to know that it is time for sleep.

2. When stress and worry prevent you from getting good sleep: Plan ahead and take out a notepad at least an hour before bed and jot down your main concerns, and then write a few remedies you can explore. This tip may get some of the worry along with some potential solutions out of your temple before getting ready for bed. Also, make an effort to replace the worry with some thoughts of gratitude.

3. Be intentional about the kind of optional information you take in on a daily basis. Place some limits on the amounts of media and news you take in as it often bends toward problems, conflicts, tragedies and turmoil in the world. It can burden your spirit and leave you feeling overwhelmed. Make it a practice to look for nuggets of goodness. Choose to find and focus on some positivity, and as an experiment, see what positive news or information you can find to share. It's really about training our minds to find and dwell on the positive.

4. Take breaks throughout the day. Instead of going directly to your phone or social media, use break time to affirm yourself, to dwell on what's working well in your life. Positive self-talk is one of the most powerful tools we have readily available.

5. Get good nutrition. Some people 'feed' and take better care of their automobiles than they do their bodies. When you do not begin your day with good fuel for your physical body, you begin the day behind the power curve. When schedules are busy, plan ahead by keeping small snacks such as peanut butter and crackers, nuts, fruit or veggies with you so that you can nourish your body and mind with something healthy. Remember if our brain doesn't have nutrients, it is not going to be very productive or positive and this affects how the rest of our temple functions.

6. Too busy to get to the gym for exercise? That happens. However, during the day you can still get in some exercise. Do some stretching, run in place for five minutes, some lunges, push-ups, or squats. Be creative and focus on ways that you can strengthen your body when you do not have time to get to the gym.

The strategies that Felicea shared on taking care of our mind, body and spirit show highly impactful, yet doable actions. We may be doing a great job in nurturing one or two dimensions of the temple God gave us. But it's worth an assessment for a few weeks to see what area(s) we may be neglecting.

One of Felicea's associates summed things up this way; "Whenever I'm feeling kind of emotional about something or maybe I'm not about to make the best choice as it relates to my nutrition, or I skipped a workout, I try to check myself and ask, Is what I am about to do going to bring honor and glory to God?" If she answers yes, then she moves forward with that decision. But if her answer is no, or not a clear yes, then she chooses a different path, or a different snack or a different action.

Felicea Myer-DeLoatch made the case for the importance of caring for ourselves holistically. She presented simple and practical ways to become intentional with steps to enhance the care of our mind, body and spirit. We can begin with one idea and practice it until it becomes a habit and then add another and then another.

Building the habits that nurture the physical, mental, and spiritual dimensions of our God-given temples is a God-honoring way to live!

REFLECTIONS FOR YOU:

1. What aspect of what Felecia described resonated most with you?

2. What part(s) of your self-care (mind, body, spirit) need more attention?

3. What is one idea or action from this story that you are willing to adopt into your self-care routine?

LIVING IN THE MIDST OF A MIRACLE - MEL AND CECELIA MANN

The Lord sustains them on their sickbed and restores them from their bed of illness. (Psalm 41:3)

From the outside looking in, or at a glance, Mel and Cecelia Mann, along with their young adult daughter Patrice, appear to be an ordinary happy, close-knit family. And they are, but they certainly experienced a season where life literally stopped them in their tracks.

First, a little background on the couple. Mel was raised by a single Mom along with his two older siblings in Cincinnati, Ohio, a large urban area. Quite the opposite, Cecelia Mann grew up with her parents and siblings on a farm on the edge of Phenix City, Alabama, a small town where she and her siblings had the freedom to roam and explore safely. She was the third of six children. After a whirlwind courtship, Mel and Cecelia married in November of 1984. Mel was active-duty Army and the family moved six times for his different assignments. Mel, Cecelia and their daughter Patrice share the core values of education as a high priority. In addition, service to others, being active in their church, recreation, humor and balancing the mind, body and spirit are also very important.

Mel loved running since he was a teen. At 15, he qualified for the Boston Marathon with 20 minutes to spare, but he was too young to run it, as the minimum age was 18. In high school Mel was the captain of his track and cross-country teams. Growing up Cecelia enjoyed sewing, hanging out with friends and family, board games and the 4-H club. Today she enjoys bridge, fun runs, sign language, photography, gardening, and is an avid reader (being a member of several book clubs).

It was the Christmas season of 1994. The Manns lived in Michigan and had traveled home to Phenix City, AL for the holidays. But before Mel left, he had an MRI test done because of a pain in his back. They had a wonderful time with Cecelia's family and returned home to Michigan full of holiday cheer. On the way to work the next day, he went by the clinic to get the MRI results. That's when he was hit with some unbearable news. At 37 years old, when he and Cecelia had been married ten years and their daughter was only five years old, he was diagnosed with chronic myeloid leukemia. Mel's prognosis was terminal, and he was given three years to live. Mel's doctor told him that his only hope was a bone marrow transplant. And even if he found a bone marrow donor that matched, the procedure was still very risky. His body could reject the donor's marrow with a fairly quick death to follow. Use your imagination to let this real-life scenario that the Manns faced sink in for a moment.

Mel described being in shock. He remembers hearing a loud ticking sound in the doctor's office which was the wall clock ticking. He described feeling like he was under water as he sank down into the couch in the doctor's office. Cecelia recalls Mel returning home, such a short time after he left, that she thought he had forgotten something. But when he walked in the house, his face was so solemn, she knew something was wrong. When he delivered the news that he had cancer, she, like him, went into shock. Cecelia remembers it was such a huge blow, the whole world stopped.

So that was what the Manns were facing - a terminal diagnosis, and the need for a bone marrow donor match to save Mel's life. It turned out, not only were none of his family members a match, but nobody on the national registry matched his bone marrow type. And there were no drugs, nor any therapies.

However, Mel and Cecelia were people of faith. Many people of faith find it easy to have faith when things are going well in their lives. But what about when you are tried in the fire like the Manns? What did Mel and Cecelia do? They prayed to God and were sure that He knew their circumstances. They decided to do what they could do and to trust that God would do the rest.

Mel and Cecelia began researching bone marrow transplants. A transplant as a cure for cancer was quite new to them. Having been told there was no match, Mel decided he would have to go out and find his own match. Subject matter experts advised Mel against searching for his own donor match, instead he was advised to save his energy for dealing with the diagnosis. But that's not what the Manns felt led to do. As they began their research, they found out there weren't many people on the registry. Mel and Cecelia set about getting ready to educate people on the need for marrow matches, to start some bone marrow drives and to help build up the registry for bone marrow donors. They believed that was their part to do and that God would deliver the rest.

Mel and Cecelia held on to their strong faith in God and

they were blessed on the journey. Mel contacted the Red Cross, stating he wanted to start doing some marrow drives. They sent him responses that no one had ever found their own marrow donor. They too suggested that Mel should spend his time adjusting to the general medical treatments.

However, the Red Cross noted that if he wanted to go ahead with the drives, they would work with him. Mel had requested a second opinion from the Walter Reed Army Medical Center in Bethesda, Maryland. While there, he went by the Department of Defense's Marrow Foundation. He then shared his desire to start doing some marrow drives. Mel sensed this was his calling and that there was some reason that he had this particular illness, not some illness that he could fight quietly and emerge triumphantly. So, he dedicated his faith and time to these marrow drives. At the first drive, 350 of Mel's co-workers stepped up to give a small amount of blood to see if they were a match. Today the test is much easier and quicker: a cheek swab only. Back then, 22 years ago, the marrow drive could take a whole day because of the time required to draw blood samples.

Mel subsequently got involved in some very large marrow drives, including a world record breaking 10,000-participant drive held at Fort Bragg, NC and it took a whole week for all the participants to be tested. Mel initiated and participated in marrow drives for three years. However, at the end of three years, he still had not found a donor.

Fortunately, he was at a drive later on and guy who had seen him on television advertising for the drive came up to him. The gentleman told him that the drives were great, but he recommended that Mel go to MD Anderson Cancer Center, in Houston Texas. This gentleman, who had leukemia too - although a different type - said he had been near death, but was brought back to life by MD Anderson. The gentleman gave Mel the phone number to the MD Anderson Cancer Center. When Mel called, he got to speak with a doctor and a nurse, as they both picked up the phone! He later learned that all calls were routinely answered by the Leukemia front desk. The doctor and nurse told Mel it was the first time either of them had answered that phone line directly in 20 years. Wow!

MD Anderson told him to come out to Houston, TX, their Headquarters at the University of Texas Medical Center. There, the doctor reviewed Mel's records very carefully. The doctor proposed they put Mel on one experimental drug after another to fight the disease aggressively. By the third year of his three-year prognosis period, Mel had been a part of two unsuccessful clinical trials where he had stayed at MD Anderson for a nine-week period at a time. By now, Mel had become frail. Even after a full nights' sleep he would wake up feeling as if he had not had any rest. He was becoming too weak to do almost anything. Although he was frail, Mel would still attempt to run. By early 1998, Mel had difficulty even running one block.

Mel went to his doctor asking about more drugs. The doctor mentioned there was this one drug, but it was still in testing and it was not yet approved to be tested on humans. Finally, about eight months later, MD Anderson got the approval to begin using the new drug, Gleevec. Mel was now eight months past the three-year mark. He was the second person to begin using

Gleevec at MD Anderson. The drug slowly started changing Mel's bone marrow back to normal. It put his leukemia into complete remission!! Amazing!!

Currently, Mel is the longest living person in the world on the drug, Gleevec. He still takes the drug today as a maintenance treatment. The drug turned what was a fatal disease into a chronic disease. How soon did Gleevec begin working for Mel? Remember Mel's love of running? Mel began taking the drug in August of 1998 and by June of 1999 he was completely back up to speed and ran a 26.2-mile marathon in Anchorage, Alaska; quite a miraculous recovery!!

Mel recalled a time in the waiting room at MD Anderson when he saw a woman who was in a wheelchair. She was on the same clinical trial that he was on. He remembered one day this same woman walking out of the doctor's office, almost knocking him over. When he realized this was the same woman who had been in the wheelchair, Mel knew that this drug was going to work.

How did the Manns keep going for the three years and eight months before Gleevec was prescribed for Mel? It was their faith. They continued to pray and believe. They had friends, family and their church community praying and encouraging them. Mel and Cecelia could not over emphasize how much participating in the marrow drives and the recruitment and education of others helped them; it calmed their anxieties and gave them something to focus on. Their perspective was not only that the bone marrow drives could possibly help Mel, but they could definitely help other people. The Manns felt that was what God wanted them to do. While Mel did not receive a bone marrow match, there were other people that did, and their lives were saved. It brought joy to the Manns to hear those success stories. They continued on that path and held onto hope until Mel received the incredible blessing of a successful clinical trial that was nowhere in the makings when he was diagnosed.

Their faith helped Mel and Cecelia to stay calm, which is important in any struggle. Their faith gave them hope, and hope is definitely needed when one is dealing with cancer. The couple worked to maintain a normal life throughout this ordeal. Many who learned of Mel's story after his condition became manageable with Gleevec had no idea what he was going through. The successful clinical trial allowed Mel to continue his hobbies and even go back to school. The Manns opted for Cecelia to be a full time Mom in order to ensure a stable environment for Patrice, particularly when he had to take extended trips to MD Anderson, where young Patrice sometimes thought Daddy was gone on vacation.

As the Manns look back and reflect on their season of 'trial by fire,' Cecelia acknowledges that it was surreal sometimes to think about Mel still being here, still heading their family. It has made every anniversary and milestone that happens in Patrice's life a wonderful moment of celebration! Cecelia sees her family as living in the midst of a miracle!

Thus, their message is to just never, never give up faith. From his experience, Mel realized how critical it was to never take away anyone's hope, no matter what they were going through. He made sure to keep others encouraged and to give them hope as only God knows the future. Mel agreed that they are living in a miracle. He has felt blessed, and he saw the hand of God throughout the entire challenge. He recognized that it rains on the good and the bad so that while you prepare for the worst, we must always hope for the best. His word to others is, "stay strong, keep your head up and keep moving because you never know what tomorrow will bring."

The Manns have learned and lived that when you are faced with a major challenge and you're praying to God, sometimes you ask Him for a particular outcome. But they experienced that it was important to be open to where He might take them to resolve their challenge. In Mel's case, they were advised that the only cure or way for him to live was a bone marrow transplant. That prompted them to initiate recruitment of potential donors and raise awareness on the process. The Manns felt donor drives, advocacy and patient education was what God wanted them to do then, and it is what they have continued to do now. But it turned out, God saved Mel's life through a clinical trial.

What a miraculous journey Mel and Cecelia's lives have traveled! Over the years the Manns have continued to be actively involved in different marrow drives and Leukemia & Lymphoma Society's (LLS) Team in Training and other LLS activities. They have stood in the shoes of those facing a terminal illness and want to do everything they can to help.

We have observed a powerful lesson through the Manns' story. God's law of getting back what you give out is true! It may not happen when and how we expect it, but trust, believe and have faith that it will, as it did for Mel and Cecelia. They helped to bring healing to many via expanding the bone marrow donor registry and healing came to Mel via a clinical trial.

At the time of our conversation, the Manns were looking forward, excited and proud as their daughter Patrice prepared to graduate from medical residency and the family also celebrated Mel's 60th birthday.

It's been 26 years since the day Mel received the diagnosis of leukemia. The Manns are still a happy, close-knit family and through their faith, they are living in the midst of a miracle!! Further, through their commitment to serving others, Mel and Cecelia have made and continue to make a tremendous difference in the lives of so many, as does their daughter, Dr. Patrice Mann, now a practicing psychiatrist. Great is Thy faithfulness!!

NOTE: Readers who have a desire for more information or interest in becoming a bone marrow donor, go to www. Bethematch.org.

REFLECTIONS FOR YOU:

1. What important lessons does the story of the Mann Family offer you?

2. Does your family share a few core values? How are you living them?

3. What miracles are occurring in your life that you may overlook from day to day?

A FORMULA FOR PEACE – LINDA EATMON-JONES

And the peace of God, which transcends all understanding, will guard your hearts and your minds in Christ Jesus. (Philippians 4:7)

Over the different seasons and experiences in our lives, one thing we all have in common is the need to figure out how to operate in the world and what works best for us. In some cases, whatever we have in front of us, or the memories of things that have happened in our past can take away our peace. When we face difficult situations, whether with health, family, finances, career or relationships, one thing we often crave is peace.

One dear friend created a formula that she applied time and again, so that no matter what she had in front of her to cope with, she not only had peace, but God's peace. And she is someone who never shrank in the face of any challenge, or anything she wanted to accomplish. While many of us may first ask ourselves if we can do something, it certainly does not include Linda Eatmon-Jones. Her first question to herself would be, 'what do I need to do to make this happen?' not whether or not she could do it. Linda was a smart, confident achiever, who gave and loved with her whole heart. Her wise formula to have God's peace in her life will be shared a little later and might prompt you to create a formula for yourself.

First a little of her background. Linda grew up in a small North Carolina town, just across the Virginia border. She was the oldest of five children. Linda went from elementary to high school all on the same school grounds, simply going to different buildings as she went from elementary to middle to high school. This school model proved to be a great foundation for her because she got to know and work with successful high school students before she reached high school. The high school students did more than model academic growth, they also helped Linda to hone her social and communication skills, and to develop responsibility and independence. For instance, Linda was in school bands with high school juniors and seniors as a seventh grader.

Growing up, family, school and church activities filled Linda's days. She excelled in math and science, and as an honor graduate, she wanted to become a physician, but once enrolled in college, her interest changed and she decided to get her degree in psychology. Nonetheless, Linda maintained her love of math and science and after college accepted a position in technology and finance in the Washington, DC area. She has worked and lived in the area since college. Linda and her husband Earle have a son who is a pastor and youth director. He and his wife have given Linda and Earle two beautiful grandchildren aged seven and five at the time of our interview.

Linda's core values have been pretty much the same all of her life. Having faith in God and keeping His Word; Family relationships are fundamental; Having the courage to be honest; Letting her actions speak louder than her words; Seeing the glass as half full, and lastly, Knowing the difference between doing things right and doing the right things. In addition to her core values, Linda described two common threads that have run throughout her life. First, when she gives with an open hand and expects nothing in return, she feels really blessed by God for things that she could not have imagined coming into her life! The second common thread is expressing gratitude for the small things in life. Linda showed remarkable creative talents which inspired family and friends alike who read her books, knew of her many involvements with her grand-kids, civic engagements, or who experienced the 'take your breath away' settings of the Joneses' Christmas parties.

Linda was met with a major challenge just a couple of years before our interview and she forthrightly demonstrated her core values and formula for peace. In the spring of 2014, Linda began suffering from severe rashes on her back and neck, along with swollen lymph nodes. She felt miserable, having many tests and biopsies to find out the cause. She was prescribed topical creams and antibiotics but nothing seemed to work. After nearly fainting one morning in August of that year, she was hospitalized for a week and diagnosed with Hodgkin's lymphoma, a cancer of the blood and bone marrow. During her hospitalization, it was determined that she had been living on one lung for a long time as her left lung was filled with cancerous fluid that had to be drained.

Linda felt at a low point wondering about what had transpired and what it meant for her. But again, she applied those values and what past experience had taught her. In the midst of a battle with Hodgkin's lymphoma, with a lot of uncertainty about what lay ahead, Linda saw it as a time to change her focus from herself and instead look to God. As she moved through the various stages of treatment and chemotherapy, she knew she needed to listen to God. Linda began appreciating the little things on the journey of this health challenge. Being thankful when the results from the pre-tests showed that her body was ready for chemotherapy, and never having to postpone a treatment. She appreciated having little to no side effects during treatments and she rarely felt tired like many had told her she would. She was grateful that she felt well enough to continue the work she had planned to do between chemotherapy sessions, all of the little things...each moment, each day. Linda was not focused so much on whether the treatments were working, but was just enjoying the little things in life that God gave her during her battle with cancer. Her faith even allowed her to put attention on things she might ordinarily be doing, instead of being preoccupied with having a cancer diagnosis.

Linda acknowledged that going through cancer was a major challenge in her life. She had stumbles, question marks and like any patient with cancer, she had moments of feeling the seriousness and struggle of what she was going through. But she knew she was not in the battle alone - that God was in the battle with her, and she focused on that during her daily prayers. Linda practiced gratitude, faith in God, and she continued to see the glass as half full, all of which really helped keep her going. Faith in particular, allowed her to stay confident and move forward. In fact, faith had always allowed her to get through the things she could not conquer on her own. Instead of dwelling on the struggle with cancer, Linda remembered what God had already done for her...the moment before or the day, month or year before. These thoughts prompted her to give thanks and praises for all of those blessings.

Linda's kind of faith is such a testament to its power. Not everyone has that kind of faith, yet. While many can relate to her story of going through serious health challenges, without faith they may feel alone. They may not have a relationship with Christ or know how to build their faith. Linda admitted that even believers in Christ have some days when they have doubt. She recommended prayer. As she noted, "Anyone can ask Christ to come into their life or come back into their life." Linda was confident that when we invite Christ into our lives, He will show up! Linda illustrated through her own experience of praying daily what she terms as her three Ds: direction, discernment and discipline. Linda explained her three Ds this way: "Praying for direction is to seek an answer to a problem we have or how to help someone else. We have to seriously listen to know when God is answering our prayers. That's why I pray for discernment, so while I'm listening, I can see and hear what God is saying and be able to separate His Answer from worldly answers. Discipline then allows me to be astute because God speaks to us in many different ways. You have to pay attention for the answers you ask of Him. Sometimes the things you ask for may appear, but it may be through somebody else or when you're parking your car or it may just be right in front of you. And sometimes it's praying for the discipline to refocus myself on what he wants me focused on."

So, what was Linda's formula for peace? It has brought her through life's challenging situations just as described with the health challenge she faced and many others. It has allowed her to keep moving forward, over and over again. Linda's formula is: *Prayer + Gratitude = Peace.*

What a simple but powerful formula to face any season in life and still find peace!! If you are unsure of how to find peace in your life and your circumstances, Linda's story has shown you one formula that works. Begin a relationship with Jesus Christ through prayer (talking to Him) and study His Word. Find a translation of the Bible that you can understand. And then pay attention and be grateful for the blessings and small things, the things that are working well now, and the things that He has already brought you through in your life. Remember, *Prayer + Gratitude = Peace.*

As our conversation was about to end, Linda shared a beautiful analogy pertaining to the relationship believers have with God. She used her relationship with her precious grandchildren, Ryan and Rachel whom she so enjoys spending time with. She described how God has His eye on the sparrow (us) the same way she watches over her grands. They never have to worry, because they know Grammy is there for them. That's the way God is with us. He is looking out for us and taking care of us every day, to the point where we do not have to worry about our needs. We can be carefree like children and not worry, because just the way that Linda is as a Grammy for her grandchildren, God is that way looking out for all of His children.

NOTE: Linda Eatmon-Jones had a recurrence of cancer in 2020 and the Lord called her home. She is deeply missed, but her love and light live on through her family and those privileged to know her. I am one of the privileged who got to call her Soror and friend. There were so many qualities to love and admire about Linda. She was one of the people who encouraged me to get this book that you're reading from an idea to a finished book! I thank God for using Linda to be such a bright light in this world, and for all of her generosity, inspiration and love!! Her life glorified God and now she rests in Heaven.

REFLECTIONS FOR YOU:

1. How did you relate to Linda's formula to find peace?

2. How much of a role does gratitude and prayer play in your daily life?

3. What disturbs your peace? What do you do to resume a peaceful state?

TRUSTING GOD DESPITE THE ODDS –
JANICE LAVORE-FLETCHER

The righteous cry out, and the Lord hears them; he delivers them from all their troubles. (Psalm 34:17)

Picture this in your mind's eye. A doctor sees results of tests you have taken and tells you that you have a brain tumor and that there is nothing they can do. Close your eyes for a moment and think of hearing a doctor tell you to go home and get your affairs in order. Wow. What must go through the mind of a person who is given such a report from a physician? Janice LaVore-Fletcher experienced that exact scenario, and we'll see how she handled it.

Janice is the Founder and President of the Christian Coach Institute in Charlotte, North Carolina. She and her husband Dale, who is also featured in this book, have four adult children. And today in 2021, they also have a beautiful grandson Judah. Janice is the eldest daughter of seven children, raised by a loving, strong, faith-filled Mom. From the time she was a young girl, she was interested in teaching. She would get her brothers and sisters or anyone else, to include the family dog or cat to let her teach them something. Janice always enjoyed mentoring and helping others along. As the oldest daughter, she saw herself as the leader and the caregiver, teaching and training everyone in some type of way. In high school she had her first class on psychology which lit her up and ignited her interest in human behavior. She remained fascinated by human behavior which led her to adult education, training and development, leadership, coaching and development.

Janice lives by five core values: excellence, Christ-centered, authenticity, relationships and integrity. As Janice spoke about her life, core values, her love of family and friends, successful corporate career, and her passion as the head of the Christian Coach Institute, her life sounded fulfilling and rewarding. But where in her life story did a doctor tell her the unthinkable, 'there's nothing we can do?'

In October 2000, Janice faced the most challenging period in her life. At the time she had an executive corporate position and things were truly well by the world's standards. Then she was diagnosed with a brain tumor and was told there was nothing that could be done. Doctors told her it was inoperable, that the tumor was wrapped around the main artery in her brain and it could snap at any time, and that she needed to get everything in order. Janice pursued other medical opinions and she even experienced one doctor becoming agitated by her queries for any options, telling her "You are in denial, don't do this to yourself or to your family. Go home, get your affairs in order. There's nothing we can do." This devastating type of diagnosis could likely shorten a person's days because they lose all hope.

So, what did Janice do? She trusted God despite the odds. She felt God's presence and held on to her faith. Janice knew that the prognosis she had been given were the words of man. She knew that God was saying he had more for her and she knew that God loved her. The depth of this challenge moved her to truly "let go and let God." Janice decided that no matter what the outcome, she would stay totally dependent on God.

Janice lived in Florida and recalls a beautiful affirming moment of her faith during this most challenging time. It was during October and she was planting flowers. Her mother and son left her planting as they went to get mulch. As she planted the flowers, Janice prayed for courage, to be strong for her son, and for him to see that her faith was real. As she prayed, she heard a buzzing overhead. She looked up wondering what the noise was. It turned out it was a skywriting plane and he had already written in the sky, *God Loves,* and just as she looked up, the skywriter was finishing the letter 'U'. Janice felt that *"God Loves U"* message was for her. She claimed it and she hung on to that message over the duration of that difficult season.

Over a period of two weeks through God's direction, Janice was led to the Chief of Neurosurgery at Massachusetts General Hospital, where they took her case and were willing to operate. When she went in for her surgery, they asked if she believed in the power of prayer. That question comforted her spirit, because she did indeed know the power of prayer. Janice had several members of her amazing family and her mother, who was her spiritual mentor, there praying with her and pointing her to assuring scriptures such as Psalm 91: 1-2, *He who dwells in the shelter of the Most High will abide in the shadow of the Almighty, I will say to the Lord, My refuge and my fortress, My God in whom I trust.* Isaiah 40:31, *But they who wait for the LORD shall renew their strength; they shall mount up with wings like eagles; they shall run and not be weary; they shall walk and not faint.*

Janice knew that her faith and the fact that people were praying for her made all the difference.

Janice's surgery was completely successful!! She was able to fully resume her previous activities and lifestyle. Although she had experienced a season of tremendous challenge, it had also been a time of renewal, and a time of refocus. Janice assessed that God was calling her to something different. As a result, she never went back to her corporate position. God told Janice that He had more for her and He opened the doors. Janice had a passion for the emerging field of professional coaching, but found that the concepts had more of a new age approach centered around the humanistic model of "I can do all things in my own strength." But for Janice, there was an obvious critical component missing which is taught in Scripture, *I can do all things through Christ who strengthens me.* Philippians 4:13. Ultimately, Janice decided she would include her Christian values and faith in the coaching process with her clients and to complete formal Christian Coach training.

As the Master Trainer at the Christian Coach Institute, Janice takes her coaching students through a robust and professional coaching curriculum with Jesus Christ and a biblical foundation at the center of it. She is devoted to and lovingly prepares students to begin careers or establish businesses and ministries as Certified Professional Life Coaches.

While Janice is busy fulfilling professional and personal pursuits, given her life's journey, how does she step away for renewal periodically now? Janice recognizes the need and value of stepping out of her work self. She loves the scripture as a reminder in Psalm 46 that says, *Be still and know that I am God.* Honoring that scripture is a way of her unplugging and going back to God, taking a true Sabbath on Sunday. Janice acknowledges the 'Martha' in her and that it's easy for her to sometimes slip into trying to get in one email or just one activity. She and her husband discuss and try to stay committed to unplugging from social media, honoring their sabbath and enjoying a day of rest and renewal on Sundays.

When Janice takes a true Sabbath on Sundays, she feels present. There is a holistic mind, body, and spirit connection. She can be more engaged with her husband. She finds herself thinking more about family and friends, connecting and worship. She becomes more energized mentally and feels better physically. Janice points to Matthew 11:28 as the perfect basis for taking a Sabbath. *Come to me, all you who are weary and burdened, and I will give you rest.* Again, Janice is not always successful with getting still and unplugging on the Sabbath, as she admits that she struggles with it sometimes, but she works at it. She also shared that one of her fun simple pleasures is enjoying God's beautiful creation. She and Dale and their fur baby, Gracie, spend many hours in their backyard growing flowers to attract butterflies and hummingbirds. And, if you happen to pass by the backyard on one of those Sunday afternoons, you would probably find Janice swinging in the hammock that her husband sets up for her and in the distance the lyrics play; *"And He walks with me and He talks with me, And he tells me I am His own, and the joy we share as we tarry there, none other has ever known..."*

Fellow believers in Christ can find Janice's remarkable story of faith uplifting and affirming when they face their own trials, trusting that God can do for them what He did for Janice. But what about someone who does not yet know Christ? What would Janice say to someone who is inspired by her trust and faith, but does not yet have a relationship with Christ? Janice responded, "Christ wants everyone to have everlasting life. He is there. All you have to do is just start talking to Him. Some people think that in order to pray, we have to stand on a pulpit and say these big, extravagant prayers, but that is not true. You come just as you are. You don't have to clean up and be perfect. And sometimes a person may think, I'm not good enough to talk to him or I have to clean up my act. But that is not true either. Even as Christians, we fall down all the time. Christ loves you and He is wooing you to His heart. All we have to do is talk to Him and ask for His help." Janice suggested picking up a Bible at a bookstore such as the New Living Translation which has a life application.

Janice LaVore-Fletcher's faith drove her to trust God despite the odds. According to certain doctors, her faith challenge was grim. But those doctors did not have the last word in her case - God did. Janice's personal philosophy in life is to learn, grow and share until she takes her last breath. Her favorite quote by Erma Bombeck, illuminates her philosophy beautifully. "When I stand before God at the end of my life, I hope I have not a single bit of talent left and can say I used everything you gave me." Glory to God!!

REFLECTIONS FOR YOU:

1. How does Janice's story speak to you personally?

2. Have you ever had the experience of trusting God despite the odds? If so, what did you learn?

3. How do you step away to renew yourself periodically?

CHAPTER FOUR

OVERCOMING UNCERTAINTY AND RISK

THE POWER OF FORGIVENESS - ALIA WATKINS

Be kind and compassionate to one another, forgiving each other, just as in Christ God forgave you. (Ephesians 4:32 NIV)

Imagine you're in a marriage where to the external world and even to your close family and friends, you've kept up a façade of what you'd once dreamed of: a happy marriage, and a wonderful life together. But inside the marriage, your dreams are shattered, really from the onset. Your marriage has become a place of dark days, with many tears. You are devastated and paralyzed, wondering "how in the world did I get here?" Yet to the world for 12 years, you continually wear a brave 'everything is fine' face. No one knows what you're really going through.

How does one move forward in a situation like this? What happens when everyone sees you as having it all together, but deep down you're facing a major life challenge? Where do you turn? This is Alia Watkins' story. Looking back at this season of her life 20 years later, Alia discussed creating a formula that she lived by and still does to this day. It has helped and equipped her to handle and push through hard times. That formula is F to the third power: *Favor + Faith + Forgiveness = Love.*

From as early as eight years old, Alia recalls hearing, feeling and believing in her heart that Jesus loved her. Alia's early introduction and acceptance of Christ grounded her for what was to come in that particular season, and in fact, for every occurrence in her life. Realizing that His presence was always with her, she was equipped to be victorious, even in the most difficult circumstances. She remembers and can relive that feeling of falling in love with Jesus. She considers His entering her life so early as His favor. The kind of life events she experienced turned on the faith switch.

Just a few of the instances of Alia having faith and receiving God's favor include growing up in a family of five children and wanting to go to college but not knowing how it would happen. But she had faith. She believed and felt a knowing that it would happen. Alia applied to schools, and as application deadlines drew close, one day a teacher who had never taught her but knew of her and her academic record offered to help her pursue an academic scholarship to Talladega College. She felt the favor of being identified by that teacher, and she received a four-year academic scholarship to Talladega College. Something similar played out for Alia to further her education after graduating from college. She had not yet decided her next move, when unexpectedly one morning, she received a call from a college professor at her Alma Mater about a fellowship opportunity to work on her Master's degree. What a blessing! After finishing her Master's, Alia again had God's favor to begin her federal career at Robins Air Force Base. These were just a few imprints of faith and favor that affirmed God's love for her. She had experienced how He could make a way out of no way and that He had specific plans and purposes for her life.

Alia got married a year after graduate school and started her federal career. But her marriage turned very painful very fast. She not only experienced difficulty and challenges inside the relationship, but there came an instance when she was even physically attacked by a woman involved with her husband. The woman came to Alia's home with the intent of attacking her - and attack her she did! Upon arriving home from an errand and exiting her car, she was assaulted without warning and was cut on her face.

Up to the time of this attack, Alia had kept the burden of her husband's illicit affair private. But now, after the attack, she was left with a visible 'battle scar' on her face for all to see, an injury that she would somehow have to explain. This incident alone might have broken others or been too much to bear. However, Alia found the strength to push past her hurt, past her disappointment and embarrassment to continue moving forward. But how?

Although this was the perfect opportunity to "out" the affair and leave the bad marriage, somehow Alia believed for her infant daughter, she should continue to try to make a happy home. Having grown up with divorced parents herself, she did not want that for her daughter. So, she continued with the façade, and merely told people a partial truth: that she had been attacked by a "crazy woman on drugs" while leaving the store. Close family members knew the whole story, but no one else. Even in this situation, Alia saw God's favor in her life. The plastic surgeon on call in the emergency room that night was thought to be the best in the state. He promised her that the scar would be barely visible. And while she still has the scar, unless you look very closely, it is hardly noticeable.

Alia kept returning to her memories from childhood about God's love. She still felt how much Jesus loved her and knew that although her current situation was very challenging, she was worthy of love. She meditated on the favor placed upon her life, all of the good people God put in her life during those hard times, her birth family, church family and work family. Every day during those painful times of her marriage, Alia intentionally found something positive that she could dwell upon. She looked forward and focused on interacting with the loving people in her life. This gave her the faith and hope that everything would be okay.

Ultimately, when she felt she could not talk to anybody else or couldn't let anyone else in, it was her personal relationship with the Lord that really got her through it all. Although others were actually there for her, she could not bring herself to open up. Because of her faith, she knew even then that she could always run and jump into the arms of the Lord without any judgment. She could ask Him to help, and every time she asked, He did. Time after time, God gave Alia the strength to keep moving and that caused her faith in Him to increase more and more. It was not easy, but God saw her through these dark times. Alia also focused on the fact that God had given to her a beautiful daughter, so it was not just about herself. She had to keep moving forward for her daughter and she did.

So, when did forgiveness come into Alia's formula? It turns out forgiveness was integral to her fully moving forward. Before she practiced forgiveness, she acknowledged she had built up bitterness and resentment toward her husband. Even though she had the courage to push through every workday and appear strong, when she returned home, it was a different story. Alia turned into a person who she eventually did not like anymore. She built up bricks around her heart and it was not good for her or for her child. Even though most of her anger and frustration toward her husband came out while she was behind the closed doors of her home, those feelings eventually started to leak out for others to see. She remembered a specific instance during an event at her daughter's school when she snapped at her husband in such an ugly way that a friend confronted her about how mean she had been to him. That moment touched her and forced her to look at herself. What she saw during her state of unforgiveness was not a pretty sight. At that moment, Alia made a decision to work on herself and to forgive.

Once Alia forgave her husband and asked his forgiveness, she had an incredible awakening! Alia thankfully recognized a significant difference in herself than when she was holding the resentment, bitterness and unforgiveness. Once she opened her heart, she decided she no longer wanted to live like that. She was no longer held captive by the hurtful events that had occurred in her marriage. She was no longer a prisoner. Alia tore down the walls she had built around her heart and she began to feel free, free to love, and free to just enjoy life again. And beyond that, it freed her for something she had no idea was going to happen. Forgiveness freed her to operate in the purpose of God! Alia was free to authentically share the Lord with others without operating privately in ugliness or ungodly ways. Alia's life transformed after the process of forgiving and asking to be forgiven. She found real peace after forgiving her ex-spouse as well as the person who left her with the scar. She admitted that forgiveness is a process, and it does not necessarily happen immediately. For some it may happen sooner than later, but anyone should be cognizant that it is a process, and one has to choose to begin the process.

Some people of faith view forgiveness as step one in the process, and reconciliation as step two. Alia believed reconciliation should be the absolute goal for those who bear the name Christian. She shared the steps she took and offered them to anyone who wants to be forgiving:

Step 1 – Admit that you are hurting yourself when living in unforgiveness.

Step 2 – Admit that you are also hurting everyone around you.

Step 3 – Realize that you are not perfect, and therefore need God's forgiveness.

Step 4 – Recognize that if you expect/want God's forgiveness, you too must forgive others.

Step 5 – Make a conscious, (out loud?) decision to forgive. It feels so liberating!

Step 6 – Ask the Holy Spirit to guide you with the instructions for how to truly forgive.

And reconciliation directly aligns with Christians striving to be Christlike. Alia pointed to what Jesus did for mankind by dying on the cross. She defined reconciliation as forgiving and then being ready to walk in a place of forgetfulness about what occurred in the past. Forgetfulness applies in the sense that you may not literally forget the harm against you, but that is no longer what you see when interacting with those who hurt you. Reconciliation is the restoring of a cordial relationship with someone. And it's the ability to interact with that person without reliving the hurt. It's the same way that Jesus interacts with us every day of our lives. Reconciliation is not easy to achieve. And sometimes, it may not be possible. The events might have been too horrible; perhaps one party could be ready to reconcile while the other party is not ready or willing to do so. In other words, one person does not have the final say as to whether or not you will be reconciled in a relationship. Alia is thankful that God wired her for reconciliation. Alia and her husband were divorced eleven years after the period when she was attacked. And her ex-husband sadly passed away seven years after the divorce. Prior to his death, Alia did take the opportunity to reconcile with him, and she also made the decision to reconcile with the person who scarred her face and they remain in cordial relationship today.

Given the challenging season she had faced, when asked to identify the common theme in her life of her life, now in her mid-50s during the interview, Alia went back to a part of her formula. Favor has been the common theme of her life. She sees how the hand of God has always been on her life. No matter the trials, God has kept her in His favor. Reflecting back on her life today, despite what seemed like unbearable pain inside her first marriage, Alia believes God has been too good to her throughout her life to focus on the bad or negative events she has experienced. Or to allow them to paralyze and prevent her from moving forward. She believes the events of her life made her strong and prepared her to be light, hope and help through service to others. She views even her successful 31-year federal service career as being a training ground for her position right now. It helped equip her to concentrate on being a focused servant of God and to God's people.

Today Alia Watkins is in her second marriage of over 20 years. Her daughter and son-in-law are raising her smart and beautiful granddaughter. She deems this as her best season of life, as she continues to live her powerful formula of: *Favor + Faith + Forgiveness = Love*

REFLECTIONS FOR YOU:

1. What part of Alia's experiences resonate most with your life?

2. What is your perspective on forgiveness and reconciliation?

3. Is there anyone that you need to forgive? Is there anyone you need to ask for forgiveness?

4. What do you want to do differently in your life as you move forward?

TRIUMPH OVER OBSTACLES - REV. MICHAEL COPPEDGE

Have I not commanded you? Be strong and courageous. Do not be afraid; do not be discouraged, for the LORD your God will be with you wherever you go. (Joshua 1:9)

Recidivism is not just for drug addicts. This is a critical lesson learned many years ago by Rev. Michael Coppedge. If believers in Christ are not actively nurtured and disciplined in faith, they are certain to backslide, become consumed by obstacles in their path, and fall prey to worldly and immoral pursuits. Believers in Christ, just as nonbelievers, are cognizant of right and wrong, but in some instances, wrong feels good and wins out.

Rev. Coppedge, prior to becoming a minister, was living 'the life' full of whatever made him happy, which included a myriad of sinful and wretched deeds. His faith was in himself, living as he saw fit. Experiencing God was not a priority in his life. One day in 1986, he found himself stranded in Europe with no way of getting back to the United States. Think of the ramifications of this situation for a moment. This type of living and recidivism may be more common than you think.

While stranded in Europe, Rev. Coppedge, known today as "Rev. Mike," had an awakening. He felt that God snatched the blinders off of his eyes and he finally saw the adverse impact his lifestyle and choices were having, not only on himself, but on his family. Rev. Mike was so remorseful and repentant that it turned his life around. He was no longer who he had become, because he had a renewing of the mind, and was transformed and restored to a new life in Christ Jesus.

Rev. Mike was almost 40 at the time, yet spiritually he was still like the same little boy who at age seven accepted Jesus Christ as his Lord and Savior. Why? Because he had not been discipled in the faith nor had he stayed in the Christian community that would help him grow in his faith and establish a proper relationship with God as a follower of Christ.

During his early growing up years, Rev. Mike's life was challenging. He suffered low self-esteem and wanted to be anyone else but himself. You see he was the fourth born of five children which created sibling rivalry and turmoil in his life. It was difficult living in the shadows of his two older sisters and an older brother. Also, when his baby brother came along, everything came very easily to this younger sibling. As a consequence, Rev. Mike felt he had to fight for any recognition and attention that he received.

The family did not have a lot of material things, but they had a loving mother and all that they needed. Rev. Mike's father was a 30-year career Navy man. Because of his father's extended time at sea, Rev. Mike felt estranged from him for most of his developmental years. It wasn't until his father retired from the military that Rev. Mike established a positive and loving relationship with him. However, by that time, he had graduated from high school and was away in college and living very much in the world on his own.

Rev. Mike was raised in a Christian home and had accepted Christ at the age of seven. But growing up, he had a rough time trying to figure out how to be a Christian man, and how by his own devices to succeed, be joyful and content in life. Somehow deep inside, Rev. Mike knew, like many of us know today, that you cannot outrun God. But he refused to be obedient and submit to God's will and purpose. He was going in the opposite direction. Hence, Rev. Mike's belief that recidivism is not just for drug addicts. Without spiritual guidance, active nurturing and discipling in the faith, he found himself constantly being disciplined by God and man for making sinful choices. And this can happen to anyone.

Fortunately, after Rev. Mike's awakening in 1986, he realized he needed to fully surrender to Christ and allow Him work things out in his life. And that was what God did! First, God made a way out of no way for Rev. Mike and his family to return to the United States. And then, lo and behold, in December 1991, Rev. Mike was called into ministry, to teach and preach God's Word, to make disciples, and minister to God's people!

Rev. Mike described two things as his greatest lessons from this period of his life-changing challenge. The first lesson was to be obedient to God's Word. That required him to study and meditate on God's Word. He had to put on a new set of lenses to start reading between the lines in order to understand what God was telling him. He discovered it best after reading the Word, to not just close the bible and walk away, but to meditate on God's word in order to grow a personal relationship with Him. The second lesson was Rev. Mike seeking to live out the plan that God had for his life.

Rev. Mike had some fundamental strengths and values

(honed from his mother) that equipped him for his journey in ministry right up to the present. His strengths are his dependability, loyalty, honesty, optimism, open mindedness and his passion about the things he gets involved with. Rev. Mike also embraces being respectful of others, not just those in authority, but everyone, and simply loving everybody. His core values which still drive his life today are his belief in God, the fundamental importance of family, good stewardship of resources, trust has to be earned, and a healthy work-life balance.

Only God could equip Rev. Mike with these strengths and values, essential for the work He has already purposed for him to do. Rev. Mike views his primary call within the church to carry the gospel to the outermost parts of the earth based upon the Great Commission given the global Church in Matthew 28:19-20: *Therefore, go and make disciples of all nations, baptizing them in the name of the Father and of the Son and of the Holy Spirit, and teaching them to obey everything I have commanded you. And surely, I am with you always, to the very end of the age.*

Rev. Mike feels passionately that believers in Christ are commanded to go outside the walls of the church and wherever it may be, locally or globally, to share the Good News of Jesus Christ. He believes; "Once people accept Christ as Lord and Savior, we are to make disciples of them so they can likewise go and do the same for others." It is noteworthy that only God's grace and mercy allowed Rev. Mike to live through the consequences of not having his faith nurtured and not steadily growing his relationship with Christ to arrive at this point in his life.

Could his personal experience have helped Rev. Mike appreciate the need for believers to have continual growth of their faith and understanding God's Word, and the need to immerse themselves in a community with other believers? Yes, Rev. Mike's personal experience prepared him to understand that believers have to lean on someone other than themselves or other people. There are things beyond intellect, our knowledge, skill and abilities, things that we can't accomplish or do on our own. We have to learn to surrender those things to God who is Sovereign and all powerful.

What ultimately was Rev. Mike's greatest obstacle and how did he deal with it? He realized he had been his own greatest obstacle because he was not focused on God's plan for his life, but on his own plan. His Mom taught him that when faced with an obstacle or adversity in life, to check yourself first. Although Rev. Mike hasn't always done so, he now readily examines himself seeking clarity, and then turns to God. He meditates on Psalm 139:16 that says, *your eyes saw my unformed body; all the days ordained for me were written in your book before one of them came to be.* Rev. Mike knows that any obstacle he faces has not caught God by surprise and neither should it take him by surprise. There is a purpose or lesson to be learned from the obstacle. Rather than moaning or groaning about an obstacle, Rev. Mike now focuses on learning the obstacle's lesson and getting back to God's plan for his life.

A few of Rev. Mike's favorite scriptures to meditate on to stay focused when he faces obstacles are below:

Psalm 37:25 - *I was young and now I am old, yet I have never seen the righteous forsaken or their children begging bread.*

Joshua 1:9 - *Have I not commanded you? Be strong and courageous. Do not be afraid; do not be discouraged, for the LORD your God will be with you wherever you go.*

Psalm 139: 1-18 - *You have searched me, LORD, and you know me. You know when I sit and when I rise; you perceive my thoughts from afar. You discern my going out and my lying down; you are familiar with all my ways. Before a word is on my tongue you, LORD, know it completely. You hem me in behind and before, and you lay your hand upon me. Such knowledge is too wonderful for me, and too lofty for me to attain. Where can I go from your Spirit? Where can I flee from your presence? If I go up to the heavens, you are there; if I make my bed in the depths, you are there. If I rise on the wings of the dawn, if I settle on the far side of the sea, even there your hand will guide me, your right hand will hold me fast.*

If I say, "Surely the darkness will hide me and the light become night around me," even the darkness will not be dark to you; the night will shine like the day, for darkness is as light to you. For you created my inmost being; you knit me together in my mother's womb. I praise you because I am fearfully and wonderfully made; your works are wonderful, I know that full well. My frame was not hidden from you when I was made in the secret place, when I was woven together in the depths of the earth.

Proverbs 3:5-6 - *Trust in the Lord with all your heart, lean not to your own understanding. In all your ways acknowledge him and he will make straight your paths.*

Did Rev. Mike ever have a vision for his life that he would someday be in ministry and travel the world for Christ sharing the gospel? No, he did not. But after his total surrender to God, Rev. Mike has been obedient, living those things that God impressed upon him to do. Consequently, Rev. Mike has trained, equipped and led mission teams to both domestic and international mission fields. Some of his international mission trips have been to Haiti, Slovakia, Austria, Uganda, Kenya, Senegal, Zimbabwe, Brazil, Russia, Italy and Antigua.

One way that Rev. Mike prepares mission teams across the globe to share the good news of Jesus Christ is through the use of a familiar scripture, John 3:16. *For God so loved the world that He gave his only begotten son, that whosoever believes in Him shall not perish but have everlasting life.* He teaches teams how to break down that one bible verse in conversations with others on the mission field.

For God: Talk about God's character; who is God? He's omniscient, omnipotent.

So loved the world: Describe the height & depth of God's love

That he gave his only begotten son: Who would give their child to die for those they do not know?

That whosoever believes in him: Just freely believe, regardless of who you are or your circumstances

Shall have everlasting life: That you will not go to hell, but you will enjoy eternal life with Him.

What a powerful tool this one scripture can be for any Christian seeking a simple way to share the good news of Jesus Christ with others!

Rev. Michael Coppedge is living the experience and testimony of how to have triumph over obstacles. As he looks forward, he is very intentional about discipling more people who will be equipped to go and share the gospel. He seeks to replicate himself, to spend more time discipling other people and impressing upon them the importance of going and fulfilling the Great Commission.

REFLECTIONS FOR YOU:

1. What obstacles are standing in the way of more fulfillment in your life right now?

2. What would be different in your life if you got rid of the obstacles?

3. Have you ever found 'you' as your greatest obstacle, the weapon formed against yourself?

4. How can Rev Mike's story help you triumph over your obstacles?

A MATTER OF CHOICES – LONNIE WILLIAMS

He will render to each one according to his works: to those who by patience in well-doing seek for glory and honor and immortality, he will give eternal life; but for those who are self-seeking and do not obey the truth, but obey unrighteousness, there will be wrath and fury. (Romans 2:6-8)

The world and our lives are full of choices each and every day. Zig Ziglar said, "You are free to choose, but you are not free from the consequences of your choice." This statement is loaded! It cautions that while you have the freedom to choose whatever you want to do, you need to be aware and intentional about your choices as they are laden with consequences. Said another way, the results or outcomes you live with in your life are correlated with the choices you make.

We can all choose to cultivate the habit of making good, smart choices in our lives. Over time we will discover the value of making certain types of choices, as we watch and experience the blessings and positive outcomes that occur. The kind of choices we make are often influenced by our knowledge and beliefs, past experiences, relatives, friends and what others are doing.

And for Lonnie Williams, his choices are also influenced by the foundation that was planted deep inside of him by a mother who always said "Just keep trusting in the Lord.' Lonnie has lived and operated under the perspective that when he comes to a fork in the road and has to make a choice, he first looks inside. That allows him to evaluate his options, and to recall what he was taught by his parents in childhood. He can recall his faith and his past experiences. Those reflections make him more inclined to make the best kind of choices when he's in a tight spot.

As you read a few snapshots from Lonnie's history and personal experiences, it may prompt you to review how you make key choices and decisions in your life. You may find some insights worth considering as you move forward.

Lonnie grew up in Houston, TX when it was still a small country town. As far back as he could remember of his childhood, he was in church every Sunday. He was active in Sunday school, the youth choir and all of the church activities for young people as he grew up. Lonnie had ample opportunities before he went off to college to become grounded in the Word of God. Lonnie acknowledged that while he was immersed in church, church was not really in him. Not yet.

At 16 years of age, in 1955, Lonnie finished high school. Although he did not have a plan to pursue college, he had an excellent GPA (only one B grade during high school). He wound up with a full scholarship to any school he wanted to attend. Lonnie had an interest in architecture and he chose to enroll at Hampton University in Hampton, VA. Lonnie still did not fully understand faith or salvation through Christ. Yet, his choices were influenced by the seeds planted in him before he left home for college. Those seeds must have been what prompted Lonnie to regularly attend chapel services on campus which encouraged him.

Lonnie recalled there were a lot of distractions at school, and a lot of chances to lose sight of getting a good education. Some of his best friends drank alcohol and smoked which he chose not to do. In Yates High School and at Hampton University, Lonnie was considered one of the "good boys." It all came down to his choices. Lonnie fondly remembered the periodic packages of goodies he would receive from home. With every box of food and supplies, Lonnie found a familiar note from his mother tucked inside that he came to rely upon. It read: "Just keep trusting in the Lord."

When Lonnie enrolled at Hampton, he was not aware that the university had a two-year requirement (freshmen and sophomores) for participation in the Reserve Officers Training Corps (ROTC) program. And if you made the right kind of grades, for your last two years, you were accepted into Senior ROTC. Lonnie made the choice to get his work done in his classes. His academic performance allowed him complete Senior ROTC, and with his performance during the Fort Knox Summer Camp, he was selected as a Distinguished Military Graduate. This honor allowed Lonnie to graduate from Hampton University with a five-year Bachelor's Degree in Architecture as a second lieutenant in the U. S. Regular Army (versus U.S. Army Reserves). Lonnie had made good and smart fundamental choices up to this point. What kind of choices did he make as he moved forward?

After completing required Basic Engineer Officer's training at Fort Belvoir, VA and more training at Fort Hood, TX, at 23 years of age, Lonnie began his first tour in Vietnam. He was exposed to some things that he never imagined seeing or experiencing, such as having your life threatened, being face to face with someone who wanted to harm/kill you, or seeing his soldier's dismembered body parts during an investigation. During his second Vietnam tour, he saw human skeletal remains piled into bombed holes in the ground where the enemy had made instant graves.

Remember when you were 23 years old? Imagine what it would be like to have a close-to-death experience at that age. Now consider having that close-to- death experience as a 23-year-old soldier in Vietnam. Within a few days of Lonnie's arrival in Vietnam, in a tent adjacent to his, a Vietcong terrorist rolled a grenade underneath the tent and killed seven U.S. soldiers. What a chilling, wake-up call for Lonnie!

He realized that but for God's protection, he too could have been killed in that same instance. Within a few days after the killing, U.S. soldiers were moved to more fortified structures. But Lonnie had begun to think about things he had never thought about before. Things such as what happened to him if he died over there. He had never really thought about whether there was a heaven or whether there was a hell. But Lonnie's close proximity to an intentional act that killed seven people, a few days after his arrival in Vietnam prompted some serious self-reflection. He began to question whether there was something that he should do better; was he doing enough? And more so, was it a matter of doing enough or was it a matter of his needing to get to know God personally? During that year in Vietnam, Lonnie told himself he needed to do something differently. There was something missing from his life and he understood he needed to direct his life more towards God. Again, it came down to choices.

The incident served as one of the transformational points in Lonnie's life. He may not have been fully aware of the impact of church or of the faith planted in him as he was growing up. But after that sobering experience, Lonnie had a shift and felt led to church everywhere he went. He chose to pray to the Lord to be with him, and the Lord was with him.

Over Lonnie's entire military career, there came one opportunity after another which reinforced the idea that he needed to get closer to God. Lonnie never faced a time where he questioned or doubted his ability to keep going, but sometimes he questioned what choices to make. Experience taught Lonnie that the choices he made with God in the middle of them, through prayer and seeking His guidance, were his best choices.

Lonnie admitted that he had his challenges with understanding some of what he watched and experienced as he tried to live a godly life. As a 2nd Lieutenant, as he tried his best to live with honesty, integrity, and morals he observed some things that really disturbed him. He knew and watched people who appeared to be living with all of the trappings of doing well, who were bad people, involved in hurting others, violence, illegal activities and low morals. Lonnie thought to himself, "why are they doing so well?" While he was making choices to live in a righteous manner, he could not understand what he was seeing. It struck Lonnie to see what looked like people getting away with their masked but corrupt lifestyles. However, in time, Lonnie came to know that God is not only good, but also a just God. He learned that the Almighty God knows our hearts and all those things that are done in pretense, as well as all of the deeds and choices that we make which are not God-honoring or morally right. It's all about our choices.

Lonnie's military assignments led to some other close brushes with harm, but each time God let him get to safety. For instance, during an assignment in Korea, his unit had to travel to the Demilitarized Zone (DMZ), the area between North and South Korea. They were responsible for maintaining all of the roads and bridges in that area. Along the way they saw crosses and flowers in honor of American soldiers who had been ambushed on that road. As they drove through the dangerous area, Lonnie remembered thinking he did not want to be represented by one of those crosses on the side of the road. He prayed and prayed. As they neared the DMZ, suddenly 22 North Korean soldiers who were dressed up as construction workers surrounded their vehicle and attacked them. Lonnie's first words were, 'Lord, help us.' He and the two other officers in a vehicle and the driver tried to defend themselves the best they could. What a realization of who God is when you are face to face and looking into the eyes of someone who is trying to take your life!

After what felt like a very long few minutes, thankfully Lonnie and the other two officers were rescued by U. S. military police who were overlooking the valley where the ambush took place. Lonnie and the others had cuts and bruises, but thankfully their lives were saved. Within a month, in the same spot, another U. S. military officer was killed. Lonnie had a grim realization, yet again, that he could have been the one who was killed. He was awarded a Bronze Star for his work in the DMZ, subjected to enemy combat. Over Lonnie's military career, he faced danger and risks to his life again and again. But God honored his faithfulness and spared his life each time.

Today, Lonnie's relationship with Christ is the very center of his life. He and his wife, Delores, have been deeply blessed to see their four sons become adults, husbands and dads who are highly successful in their chosen careers. Yet amidst the abundance of those blessings, Lonnie admits he is most grateful that his sons and his grandchildren know and accept Christ as their Lord and Savior.

There is a calmness and knowing deep in Lonnie Williams' spirit today that was not there before he made the choice to develop a personal relationship with the Lord. He lives making his life choices through prayer and "trusting in the Lord." The consequences in Lonnie's life epitomize the value and blessings of making our choices by divine guidance! We can allow our choices to be inspired by the power of the Holy Spirit who dwells within us.

REFLECTIONS FOR YOU:

1. What elements of Lonnie's story speaks to you?

2. What idea or strategy from Lonnie gives you a new insight?

3. What could be helpful for you to consider as you are making key choices about your future?

A SPIRIT OF RESILIENCE - REV. LOU PHILLIPS

And we know that all things work together for good to them that love God, to them who are the called according to his purpose. (Romans 8:28)

Early in the morning, a young boy is looking out the window of his home in Quanah, a little town in West Texas named after a Plains Indian chief, Quanah Parker. The town is predominantly Caucasian with most of the African Americans living on the other side of the railroad tracks. Everyone knew everybody in his little community, and all of the adults, all of the teachers and business folk embraced everybody's children as if they were their own. The boy's mother who headed their household, was industrious and always had some kind of business going to be able to provide for her five children and to keep them in tip top shape. Her hard work allowed her to buy a home for herself and her children near the railroad tracks.

Before the boy got up in the morning, he could hear the clickety clack sounds of the train wheels coming down the track and the train was what he was looking out the window to see. His bedroom window was close enough to the train tracks to look inside the windows of the train. He saw people in their seats reading books and he would often wonder, "where in the world are they going?" He didn't find it an interruption of his sleep, but instead, an inspiration that there was something beyond the outskirts of his little town of 5,500 people. He was determined that one day he would see what was beyond Quanah.

Minister Lou Phillips was that young boy watching the train, who wanted to know what was outside his hometown. Through his father's side of the family, he began to see some of what was beyond Quanah. All of his aunts and uncles were tremendously active in church with a number of them ministers. One uncle in particular, Rev C.J. Phillips Sr, adored him and had Lou spend summers with him in Dallas, Texas.

Lou vividly recalled and shared a few pivotal points along his life's journey once he left his hometown. Lou grew up living three core values that continued to drive him over his lifetime. First was God as the center of his universe, second was family and third was his lifelong desire even as a youngster, to be an influence and positively impact the lives of others.

After graduation from Quanah High School, in 1965, Lou entered the U.S. Army where he served for one enlistment. After he was honorably discharged from the Army, Lou worked for the City of Dallas. Then he found what began as a ticket agent position with American Airlines, which turned into a very successful 28-year career. His performance led to one promotion after another until Lou became the Director of Sales for the Eastern Region and eventually even served a stint as the General Manager of the District of Columbia's Washington National Airport. More about that shortly. Lou and the love of his life, Katherine had been married for 31 years when we spoke, and through Lou's two daughters, they were enjoying the pleasure of grandchildren. While he worked in Washington, DC, Lou was called into ministry and became an associate minister at the Antioch Baptist Church in Fairfax Station, VA.

He has traveled the world extensively, lavished his family and maintained close, loving bonds with them as well as his friends.

Lou's life and career rose on a continual positive trajectory. Does that mean Lou somehow by-passed any seasons of challenge or time in the valley? No. Lou had his share of difficult seasons, some of which he even acknowledged as self-imposed, but nevertheless, they helped him grow and develop in preparation for the particular work that he is doing now which he calls 'guerilla ministry.' Lou accepted his challenges as opportunities to operate in faith and that whatever God had him doing was for God's purposes. Lou's challenges caused him to abandon all needs and desires to feel comfortable

One example of a significant curve ball for Lou was in his career at American Airlines. He was faced with an uninitiated and unwelcomed opportunity to transition from being a marketing executive to becoming an operations leader. Lou was running a regional sales operation and received a call on Friday that on Monday morning, he was going to be the new general manager for airport operations and the Washington National Airport. Lou loved his work in marketing and sales. Suddenly he was directed to lead airport operations, something he was not well versed in, to put it mildly. He had two days to get debriefed from the outgoing general manager. Lou's immediate thought was that this opportunity was going to lead to failure on his part. Lou called to bellyache to a mentor who after listening, explained what a breadth of experience he would have after this assignment!

When he showed up as the new general manager, problems

that he had no idea how to solve were waiting for him. But Lou had faith that God would work things out. Lou fondly recalled a story he had been told years earlier when someone faced a major challenge. A guy told him, "You know we live in America, which is a free society. Throughout your life, there may be trouble. They can shoot you here, but they can't eat you because cannibalism is not allowed in America." Lou had a good laugh again at that story and it settled him down and he began to focus on the things that were important for him to be successful. He noticed God began to give him ideas and ways to improve airport operations based on the skill sets that he had gained over the years. Most of his skills had to do with focusing on employees and being an encourager. This sudden shift turned into an opportunity for Lou to live more of one of his core values of positively impacting the lives of others. He loved to do things that benefitted his employees. Eventually the people that posed the challenges upon his arrival in the new position, became his allies and gave him great support. Lou's perspective was to be resilient and to commit to accomplish whatever God put in front of him to do. In every case not only did Lou himself grow, but he had the opportunity to grow others as well.

Early on, Lou had thoughts that he would fail, or worse, would embarrass himself and his family. Lou recalls the blessing of godly counsel as he faced periods of challenge during his executive career at American Airlines and with his own company after he retired from the airlines. It helped him gain perspective and press forward even when something looked like a potential failure which would negate his past successes.

Over and over, Lou noticed that whenever he was faced with overwhelming difficulty, but he was committed to achieving the goal, God had a provision for him to succeed. He learned to slow down and look for the help he needed. And Lou always found what was needed to achieve what God wanted him to achieve.

A far more personal example of Lou and his steadfastness during a major challenge is his fight with cancer for five years. At the time of our discussion, he was in remission. But he had experienced several recurrences and understood that cancer was an ongoing fight. Lou found that his cancer battle showed him the importance of his third core value: focusing on others' needs and his desire to help others. The more Lou focused on others who were going through the same thing that he was, the less worry he had about his own journey. Lou's approach to each of his trips to the hospital for a checkup or procedure gave a clear illustration. He would go in telling everybody he was running for office. He was trying to get their vote. He told people how wonderful they were and what a great job they were doing. Even as he was getting ready to go under anesthesia for surgery, he made the

nurses feel good. He saw them as angels of mercy and wanted each of them to see themselves as a direct representation of God. He has had ministers come into his room to pray for him. Before they could walk out of his room, Lou would insist that he wanted to pray for them too. He explained that they were not just there for his situation, but that he was there for them as well. Sometimes those interactions resulted in ministers shedding tears as they saw hundreds of patients a day and rarely had one offer to pray for them.

What was this guerilla ministry Lou referred to earlier? Lou looked for ways to get into the trenches, away from the safety of being behind the church walls. He got satisfaction out of just helping folks. Like the Apostle Paul, Lou believed first was getting down on their level because you don't want to appear to be better than anybody else. Paul believed in order to grow them, he had to go down and appear to rise up with them. It's meeting people where they are, not handing down to them or looking down upon them. Lou had such a discerning and sensitive viewpoint, when he said, "Initially folks may be very suspicious as they have been Bible-thumped maybe more than once in their lives by those looking over the tops of their horn-rimmed glasses with eyes that appear more accusatory than inviting." In essence, Lou's guerilla ministry let him help those who were knocked down to look up and stand up and discover what was right before them (choices) as well as to look ahead in the distance to see what was possible for them (a future). That is resilience!

Lou believes that the quality of wanting to succeed is in everybody. No human being actually wants to fail. We all have a godly place in our spirit that we want to be the best we can be; we want to achieve. When Lou meets people where they are, he lets them see what he has done to get through the same things they are going through. As Lou establishes more of a relationship, he shares with the individuals that except for God's grace and direction and his belief that God would bring him through, living with peace and improvements would not have happened for him either.

As Lou looked ahead to the future, his focus was on continuing an initiative that he began in 2009: the IFaith Golf Cup Challenge. It's a golfing fundraiser that began for the Capital Area Food Bank in Washington, DC which grew to also include the North Texas Food Bank in the Dallas/Fort Worth area. Lou remained laser focused on helping to penetrate the issue of hunger in America, noting that 50 million people wake up every day without a clue where they would get their first meal, not to mention meals for the rest of the day. Lou had studied this issue and knew that many of the 50 million are children and seniors. With seniors, he knew they may have to make serious choices between eating and buying medication or paying their mortgage. And when children are hungry, they are not able concentrate and learn. Lou discussed a long-term strategy to coordinate similar fundraising activities in 13 different cities where 'food insecurity' is a serious factor for young and old alike.

Lou's life completely exemplified what a resilient spirit can do. He continually demonstrated an active faith and resilience no matter what challenges he faced. Min Lou Phillips went home to heaven in August 2018. He left the world a better place everywhere that he touched it. What a legacy of growing and serving! It turned out Lou lived his core values his entire life, as he remained devoted to Christ, his family and to positively impacting the lives of others. What the Apostle Paul declared in 2 Timothy 4:7 applied to Lou; He fought the good fight; he finished his race and he kept the faith. A crown of righteousness awaited him!

REFLECTIONS FOR YOU:

1. What did you find as most significant for you in Lou's journey?

2. What have you learned as you face challenges trying to achieve what God wants you to do?

3. In what areas of your life do you want to become more resilient?

BE THE CHANGE YOU WANT TO SEE: PART I – *JOANNE LATIMER*

But the fruit of the Spirit is love, joy, peace, patience, kindness, goodness, faithfulness, gentleness and self-control. Against such things there is no law. (Galatians 5:22-23)

In a visit with one of God's anointed servants, Joanne Latimer, she shared some nuggets of wisdom and sips of inspiration of how she cultivated the life of not only being a hearer of God's Word but a doer. Joanne gave thoughtful insights in a snapshot of her 60+ years journey. Maybe her reflections can encourage and enrich your life journey.

Joanne Latimer was born and raised in Gary, IN. Her character was molded early as she learned about Jesus at the age of seven. She was raised in a Christian home, where the music of gospel greats such as James Cleveland, Mahalia Jackson and Albertina Walker played regularly. Her mother and grandmother influenced her to share gifts of giving and serving. She watched both of her parents work hard, which became instilled in her as well. Joanne's parents were steadfast about being respectful and children being obedient.

Being raised in Gary, during that particular time period, after leaving the area, one question to her was inevitable, "Did you know Michael Jackson and the Jackson family?" She remembered the Jacksons when they went around doing talent shows at area high schools. Joanne recalled they appeared at her high school, at the hefty admission of 25 cents, before they were discovered.

Joanne grew up somewhat sheltered, even though they lived in a pretty safe neighborhood. As a young teen, she walked about twelve city blocks to school, to be able to participate in various activities. This was the late 1950s up to the mid-1960s. Families in the neighborhood knew each other and wouldn't hesitate to tell your parents if you were caught being too mischievous. In 1968, at 17 years of age, Joanne volunteered on Richard Hatcher's mayoral campaign in Gary where he was elected the first black mayor in a major urban city in the United States. As Joanne grew older, she began to witness the onset of the moral decline in Gary. Life seemed simple, but Joanne was little aware of the many complexities lurking around in the streets. The acceleration of drug abuse, namely heroin, had found its way into many of the local neighborhoods. Sadly, by the 1970s the inner city was infiltrated with hard drugs, and urban blight escalated.

Joanne is the mother of five daughters. Her oldest, Jameece Pinckney, also shared her story in this book. Joanne got pregnant with Jameece while in college. Against the advice of spiritual advisers, at 24 years of age, when Jameece was four years old, she got married. She and her husband David, had four more daughters. There were questionable moments before Joanne and her husband were married where she wondered if he was involved with drugs. It wasn't long before she learned the stunning truth of his addiction to heroin. Joanne's marriage slowly transformed into something unfamiliar to her. She had already been gripped by anxiety and stress, and now fear had her in its clutches too. For the next ten years, Joanne's life was riddled with episode after episode of drama, in a very trying marriage. It all culminated when she had to take the girls and quickly flee from the destructive relationship. And later, Joanne even learned that it had been reported that one of her daughters, at eight years old, was molested by her father.

Joanne's daughters were her life. Anything that brought pain or difficulty to them were the most excruciating times for her. But Joanne did not allow her seasons of trials to make her bitter or angry. Her faith kept her and her daughters through it all. She understood that all of our lives would have trials, valley experiences and suffering because it is written in God's Word. However, Joanne had the wisdom to know that it's how we translate and interpret the circumstances that make the difference in the outcome. She explained that our translation or interpretation of what's happened to us and the way we move forward validates our faith.

When Joanne's girls were young, she was determined not to go on welfare, nor leave her children to be raised by someone else. With the child support funds she received, she raised her girls and did not return to work outside the home until her youngest daughter was in first grade. Joanne kept her core values of consistency, hard work and the teachings she had received of God's faithfulness tucked away in her heart during this time.

Joanne recalled from as early in her life as age seven, prophetic words being spoken over her life. Church elders who didn't even know her would make declarations from God about her life and how she was destined to serve the Lord. Early on, their prophecies terrified her. But as many of their revelations came true, Joanne realized she had to take full responsibility for the kind of decisions she was making, and the things God called her to do. Through the wisdom of others and her first-hand experiences, Joanne's heart and mind were transformed! As she grew in faith, God used her to speak into the lives of others. Joanne absolutely trusted her spiritual gift of discernment and began to confidently speak God's Truths and operate within His Divine Order.

As Joanne's daughters became successful young adults and on their own, her life settled down. She had been a Sunday School teacher, prayer intercessor and active in a number of church ministries. But she felt led to do more. She pondered what in particular believers could do to regain spiritual control and to keep their lives intact. Joanne was led to write a book that spoke to the growing numbers of people internalizing their frustrations even to the extent that their frustrations were causing health problems. Joanne's motivation to write also came because she saw how distracted from God's Word many believers had become due to their preoccupation with their electronic devices and social media. Yet she recognized that scripture was and is still so applicable to resolve so many of today's concerns. Joanne did not write a conventional book. Instead, she followed the Holy Spirit's guidance and made it a book full of short prose; nuggets that readers can meditate on.

Early in Joanne's work on the book, she decided to address three S's in life that are common: the Stress, the Struggle and the Strain. If we are trying to pursue things in life that bring us stress, struggle and strain, more than likely, the Lord did not give us that pursuit. The Bible says in Proverbs 10:22 that the blessings of the Lord make us rich and add no sorrow with it.

Joanne conceptualized a book that would target people whose mindsets cause them a lot of dismay as they walk through their hardest challenges. The book's revelations could ultimately bring peace to the mind and peace to the heart. The Lord gave her the theme, *KISS* your mind; *K*eep your mind *I*n *S*piritual *S*overeignty. Joanne wants readers to keep the Lord in the forefront of all that they do, and all that they say. And she wants them to be gentle with themselves, as they deliberately allow the peace of God to operate in their minds.

The other critical thing Joanne wants readers to take away from the book is truth. She wisely quipped, "I don't believe in lying to myself about myself." She believes when people find excuses or a bunch of words to cover up the truth in order to feel better about themselves, that's where they start getting in trouble. In Joanne's life she has spoken and lived, "Somebody has to say the hard stuff. At least be willing to say the hard stuff about yourself to yourself." In other words, call it out, name the difficulty what it is. The fact that people are not perfect and have faults and flaws should not stop them. First is to acknowledge the challenges within their own minds and hearts. Then take it to the Lord. That puts the process of transformation in motion. Joanne reflected firsthand, "It's an amazing process to experience." Ultimately, Joanne's faith in God led her to write her book, Arai of Light, through which she brings a declaration of hope to the masses.

Joanne discussed the importance of our being doers of the Word of God, but she witnessed that sometimes we are asleep at the wheel. In other words, we miss opportunities to give and serve because we only "care from the sidelines." We may be a first step in the process by speaking on an issue. Our words and actions are seeds being planted. God will bring others to water the seeds or continue to grow the efforts. But clearly in order to 'be the change' we have to be doers and get involved. Joanne said what God gave her was, "Be a fruit dispenser." Here, Joanne referenced the Apostle Paul talking about the fruits of the spirit in the Bible in Galatians 5:22-23. Joanne personalized it beautifully by saying; "Be love, be patience, be kindness, be goodness, be faithfulness, be gentleness, be self-control. It does not cost anything to smile, use a kind voice, or to be patient with others. We don't have to grumble. When we show these attributes to others, we are dispensing the fruit of the Spirit. This is how we all can be impactful in the lives of others."

With all that Joanne has lived, given and shared, when she reflects upon what she is most proud of, it is her five daughters. Each of them fearless, smart, independent women, living full lives. Being a part of her daughters, grandchildren and great grandchildren's lives leave Joanne speechless and totally humbled. In recent days Joanne felt inspired by the Lord to be a living legacy. While it's customary to leave something behind to the family, God has inspired her to do that while she still lives. She is doing whatever she can do now to make her family's lives better, and to enrich and lift their lives in any way possible as her living legacy!

Joanne Latimer's life journey and testimony has resulted in an extraordinary impact in the lives of others. Her messages of hope uplift the troubled hearts of believers, offer peace to weary minds, and introduce the path of redemption to the lost. Her book proclaims that in the face of storms, obstacles or challenges, there is always a ray of light. She makes the people she crosses paths with or who read her book, better. Joanne is being the change she wants to see in the world!

REFLECTIONS FOR YOU:

1. What is your biggest personal takeaway from Joanne's story?

2. What is something that you feel must be changed in the world?

3. In what way can your time, energy or resources make a difference?

4. What is an area in your life where you need to tell yourself the truth?

CHAPTER FIVE

OVERCOMING WHILE SERVING

HOW DO YOU MULTIPLY? – TONY SMALL

To Him who is able to do exceedingly, abundantly above all that we ask or think, according to the power that works in us. (Ephesians 3:20)

Often at the end of the year we begin thinking about our New Year resolutions. We are eager to have a clean slate and we declare what we want to do differently in the New Year. What if you pause right now, like you might at the end of the year, to just examine where you are spending your time and energy? It's never a bad time to take one of those 'end of year' type moments no matter what time of the year you're reading this (except it may be without Christmas music or decorations.) As you look at yourself, it's worth examining how you are using the present; the time that's right in front of you, before you look ahead. A couple of essential questions for your 'end of year' type reflection might be: How can I use my gifts, time and talents to make a difference in the lives of others? How can I multiply? Why those questions? As you'll see in Tony Small's story below, your answers and follow-on actions can deepen your sense of satisfaction and blessings in your day-to-day living.

Tony Small is a highly accomplished and successful musical artist, composer, playwright and winner of national awards for his musical genius. He graduated from the Tony Award-winning BMI musical theater program which is referred to as the Harvard of musical theater. In fact, Tony was a piano prodigy who began playing at four years of age and even became a music director for his church's youth and adult choirs at the tender age of eleven. Yet with his incredible biography and accomplishments, Tony thinks that none of it means anything if we don't have God in our lives and we're not servants, nor if we do not take our gifts and give them back to impact others. He is most proud of his family, his wife of 30 years, DeJuana, also a gifted musical artist and his daughter Shana, who is a Julliard grad, and an amazing multidisciplinary artist and actor.

Tony grew up with music. His mother was a musician and sang in the choir, and he also had friends who played piano. He doesn't remember ever not having music and the arts in his life. Tony says he didn't choose music, music chose him. And his mother made him take piano lessons, but it wasn't until later that he recognized how incredibly valuable that had been. Music remained integral to Tony's life as already by his teenage years, his time was fully emersed with being a pianist to different choirs. Yet he kept training. He was the classical runner up for the state of Illinois for a piece written by Chopin.

Given his own experience with music and the arts, Tony strongly believes in the need for it in the lives of children. The fact that this type of curricula is no longer in schools drives his passion to provide the arts for kids. He explained that research has shown that the arts help children to be well balanced and to have higher self-esteem. For many years Tony has dedicated himself to providing world class arts programming to kids through his work as Regional Artistic Director of the Boys & Girls Clubs of Greater Washington. Was this Tony's dream to be involved with kids and leading arts programming for them? No, it was not.

As a matter of fact, by the time Tony headed off to college, he did not think he was going to pursue a music related degree or career. He wanted to pursue business and management, and that's where he planned to focus when he went to Anderson University. Within a couple of weeks of arriving at Anderson, someone heard him play piano and they couldn't believe he was not in the private piano class. He enrolled in the private piano class and the rest is history.

From that point on, he continued his path into music. Anderson provided him an avenue to travel the world as in a recruitment group, so at 18 and 19, he was touring the U.S., Africa and Europe with this singing group and enjoying Anderson's wonderful music training program. This phenomenal program changed his trajectory and Tony accepted that music was in fact his destiny.

Right out of college, Tony became a music teacher in a Chicago inner city school. There was not much of a budget or curriculum. They could not do musicals like Fiddler on the Roof or The Wiz because they did not have the means for the royalties or the costumes. So as the saying goes... necessity is the mother of invention. Tony started writing his own musicals and his own songs which led to some of his works becoming known and other artists wanting to record his music and do his musicals!! While that was not Tony's goal, he certainly believed that God opened doors while he was serving in the inner city, with a lot of kids that couldn't afford to pay for extracurricular activities. He felt that it was his faithfulness and dedication to what he was doing that caused doors of further opportunity to open.

Was it a tough season working with a limited budget in an inner-city school? Absolutely. Tony described this period as a particularly challenging season of life. They made some financial investment mistakes. He and his young family had limited income and were often broke. Tony and DeJuana decided to start a small music school/music business and they did not see the fruit of that endeavor for 20 years. He had lots of kids who wanted to learn how to play piano but could not afford lessons. The music school was not making any money, but he and his wife sacrificed often, at their own expense, to give the lessons and expose the children to the arts and performances in the city.

There were moments he questioned himself about what they were doing. It was a really tough time. He found himself asking, "God, are you really calling me to do this?" But in the end, he felt led, and what mattered most was the seed they were sowing into the lives of the children. Looking back, the Smalls have often reflected upon the incredible bounty they have reaped. Today those same kids have become some of the most prolific musicians across the country! Tony has renowned artists that he collaborates with today or who will agree as a favor, to teach in his music camps. Tony explained that there is no greater feeling than seeing who those children have grown up to be. He's had the blessing of seeing them *multiply* by using their gifts to teach and inspire others.

But how did Tony persevere when he was in the midst of those difficult times of very limited resources and such sacrifices in his family while working in the inner-city schools? First, Tony stayed connected to and surrounded himself with people of faith. That kept him encouraged. Tony acknowledged he would not have been as strong as he was had he not been surrounded by people of faith. It was also his own faith in God as well as his understanding of God's Word and God being able to get them through anything. Tony also created for himself an inner circle of people who were not only friends, but people who would challenge him and speak the hard truth to him when needed; such as 'Tony, you messed up', or 'Tony you need to get it together.'

Through his experience working in an inner-city school, Tony learned an essential life question: how do you multiply? It is based on the parable of the sower in the Bible - what you sow, you shall also reap. So, if you're not sowing anything, how do you expect to reap? Tony's point was whatever your passion and gifting may be, make sure that you are sowing in that arena, and he had confidence that a harvest would be the result!

Tony viewed the things that God has already allowed to happen in his life have greatly superseded his dreams. In other words, "God had already done exceedingly, abundantly above all that he could ask or think." The key question becomes, Do Tony's accomplishments, sacrifice and the bounty that he has seen returned make Tony rest on his laurels? Not at all. Every year he has goals, whether he's writing the next grant for the Boys & Girls Club of Greater Washington or looking at collaborations on some of the musical works he's done in years past. Tony sees that he will have the opportunity in the next couple of years to see some of his works performed on larger stages than he would have ever dreamed. Tony's hard work will allow him slow down and do what he calls really high-quality productions. With so many dreams realized, Tony keeps pushing, understanding that the best is still yet to come.

Given all of the opportunity and possibility for future success, how does Tony live in a space where he focuses on the present? Tony goes back to the Word of God, Matthew 6:25 which talks about not worrying about the future so much. How can any of you by worrying, add a single hour to your life… "Live in the now, or you will miss the now," Tony pointed out. He too has learned and still struggles at times, as many do, with being so focused on the future that he can miss the little, albeit important things of today. Tony's suggestion? "Plan for tomorrow but today, focus on family and lifelong friends, taking a walk outside, smelling the roses, staying connected, etc."

As a leader, influencer and mentor, Tony always ties successes with the questions, who are you pouring into? Who are you mentoring? He views being a mentor as important for paving a path or for helping others pave a path so they can hear your lessons and possibly avoid some of the same mistakes you have made.

As a final bit of inspiration, Tony shared an acronym for motivation, which he uses with the kids.

DREAM:

D - **Don't just dream; Do something** about your dream.

R - You are **Responsible** for your dream. Do not make excuses or blame others. It's up to you.

E - Make **Excellence** the very center of your character and who you are.

A - **Attitude** No one wants to work with anyone with a bad attitude. Disposition matters. Your attitude determines your altitude.

M - How do you **Multiply** your dream? You do so by giving, and by sowing into the lives of others.

The acronym DREAM can be pertinent, no matter the stage of your life.

At the time of this interview, Tony had just received notification of further recognition for his hard work from the White House Arts and Humanities Committee, an award that's a who's who of arts and after school arts programs. The recognition considers his program one of the top 50 arts programs, arts and humanities programs in the country, to be presented by then First Lady Michelle Obama!!

What's most exciting for Tony about his program receiving this prestigious honor? He's thankful and excited for the award and he recognizes the award will help them get more funding. As stated earlier, awards and accolades were never the goal, however the recognition helps more funders invest in the program. But he was most excited that the award makes it possible for him to impact more kids!

Tony's view was that "being a servant is far more than just going to church. From day to day, there are many needs in the community and we drive right past them. We pray and ask God, "What do you want me to do?" Then we drive right by someone or walk by someone who has a need. There are needs in local schools, homeless shelters and many other places in the community. What are you doing on a day-to-day basis to sow seeds? How do you multiply? You will reap a harvest, it may not be financial, but you will experience more peace and fulfillment in your life."

Tony Small's way of living beautifully captured what happens when our gifts, our passions and heart are melded together to serve others. His parting words ring profoundly true… "Doors open when you're serving, when you're giving and going above and beyond the call of duty. How can you multiply? Find a place where you can serve."

REFLECTIONS FOR YOU:

1. What is your main takeaway from Tony's story?

2. What are you doing on a day-to-day basis to sow seeds into others? How can you multiply?

3. What DREAM of yours do you need to do something about? What step toward your DREAM are you willing to take now? Then what's next?

DESTINED TO SERVE GOD'S PEOPLE –
DEACON LAWRENCE 'LARRY' HESTER

And he sat down and called the twelve. And he said to them, "If anyone would be first, he must be last of all and servant of all. (Mark 9:35)

Sometimes in our daily walk, life offers us a chance to see an extraordinary example of a servant leader up close. It's uncommon to see and it can inspire us to bend our character and actions in the direction of service to others. But first, what is a servant leader?

A servant leader is a servant first. He/she is focused on the needs of others, especially team members, before considering their own needs. A servant leader acknowledges other people's perspectives, gives them the support they need to meet their work and personal goals, involves them in decisions where appropriate, and builds a sense of community within his /her team. This leads to higher engagement, more trust, and stronger relationships with team members and other stakeholders.

Deacon Lawrence 'Larry' Hester, who served as Chairman of the Antioch Baptist Church's Deacon/Deaconess Ministry in Fairfax Station, Virginia was one of the finest examples of a servant leader that one could observe. He was referred to as Deacon Hester with great affection and respect by the entirety of his church community, many of whom had had the opportunity to have some kind of personal interaction with or support from him. This narrative was prepared from an interview with him in 2015 to honor his embodiment of servant leadership.

Deacon Hester's career background was broad; a retired Army officer, with a tour in Vietnam, a high school mathematics teacher and a highly regarded entrepreneur selling sports memorabilia through his Shortstop Baseball Card Shop. But his leadership, faith and selfless way of life were best exemplified through what he said encouraged him the most, took most of his time and that he enjoyed most and looked forward to continuing in the future - and that was serving God's people. What certainty of purpose, mission and commitment Deacon Hester had! He was totally committed to serving.

During our conversation Deacon Hester discussed some of the life challenges he had faced along his journey and how directly faith played a role in his triumphs. And we also discussed how he eventually got to his committed servant leadership. Deacon Hester's challenges began with life itself. His first three months of life were spent in Duke University Hospital where he was diagnosed with the deadly disease, diphtheria. Through much prayer and good medical care, God blessed him to recover. Growing up poor, he and his family faced the related hardships and challenges, but they kept going.

In high school he was a good student with good grades, however, he did not see how he could financially afford to attend college. But God opened a door. Deacon Hester was able to attend North Carolina A&T University and completed the Reserve Officers Training Corps (ROTC) program during college. After college, he entered the military as a 2nd Lieutenant and began a career path in the air defense artillery, a branch that had very few African American officers at the time. After retiring from the Army, Deacon Hester did something he had wanted to do; he became a high school teacher in the area school system. As much as he had a passion for teaching, as a newcomer, he was not readily embraced as a team member in the system. Nonetheless, Deacon Hester still created a way to help students succeed. He began tutoring students first at his home, and eventually through a Tutoring Ministry he helped to launch through his church, where he remained an active tutor for many years. After teaching, Deacon Hester started his own business, but faced quite a challenge finding financial support. Despite the lack of assistance or the presence of some obstacles, Deacon Hester explained that nonetheless, he always felt an obligation to excel. It was expected by his parents that he and his siblings would do well so he remained driven by that expectation. Even in the midst of struggles, Deacon Hester noted one of his attributes was his competitive spirit which drove him to put his best foot forward and to always strive to do his best.

He acknowledged that during his early years, he did not yet have God in his life. But God saw fit through His grace and mercy to allow Deacon Hester the time to get to know Him and establish a relationship with Him. Was there any pivotal moment during those years? Yes. Deacon Hester recalled a key juncture in his life after he returned home from Vietnam to a stateside assignment. In a conversation with a mentor, Lieutenant Colonel (LTC) Larry Hunsinger, it prompted him to take a long, hard look at himself. LTC Hunsinger called him one day and forthrightly asked him, "Why are you so hostile? Why are you so angry?" Deacon Hester was in fact, very hostile since he returned home from Vietnam, due to having experienced some tough and challenging situations - including the loss of soldiers. He was so angry, that as a Captain, he had made the decision to exit the military without pursuing a 20-year military career. LTC Hunsinger saw Deacon Hester's potential and promised him a command if he could bring his hostility under control. From that point he did better with managing his anger. LTC Hunsinger kept his promise and assigned Deacon Hester a command which really rejuvenated his military career. His mentor helped him see that he was holding on to things that no longer directly involved him, or which he had no control over. LTC Hunsinger believed in Deacon Hester and showed interest in him unlike he had ever experienced before. It put him on a bright path that resulted in Deacon Hester serving a full, rewarding 20-year military career to retirement.

When asked about the role faith had played in his life, Deacon Hester recalled going to church with his grandmother, but he didn't understand church because he was not taught. He was taught songs, but he was not taught scripture or how scripture had any impact on his life. He knew of God, but nothing about how to have a personal relationship with God. After marriage, his wife encouraged him and he attended church with her, and they also attended as a family during their military years.

However, after a major medical situation arose with his daughter in 1977, Deacon Hester remembered how he committed his life to Christ. There in the basement of his home, he asked God to deliver his daughter from the situation, the disease and seizures that she was experiencing. Deacon Hester promised God that he would devote his life to Him if he granted that request of healing for his daughter. God indeed healed his daughter, who now grown and married, has blessed the Hesters with two beloved grandsons. As he promised, at 31 years of age, Deacon Hester accepted Christ and he has never yielded since that commitment in 1977.

Deacon Hester was not yet committed to serve in the church, because he did not think he had anything to offer. He was blessed in 1984 to move his family to Northern Virginia, where he encountered the founding pastor of Antioch Baptist Church, Rev John Q. Gibbs. He became a member and was convinced by Rev Gibbs that he indeed had something to offer. Deacon Hester really found his niche in the church. The most enjoyable and rewarding of all the seasons of his life has been serving God's people and serving in Antioch Baptist Church.

As we discussed life challenges and faith, Deacon Hester shared that his most challenging season of life occurred two and a half years earlier. He was diagnosed with colon cancer through a routine colonoscopy in April 2013. When the doctor told him and his wife that they had discovered a tumor that could be cancerous, they looked at each other but did not panic. In fact, there was a peace abiding within them that day. The tumor was in fact cancer, and he had surgery within a few months of the discovery. The surgery was successful and by God's grace, the follow-on rounds of chemotherapy were not debilitating for Deacon Hester.

However, after chemotherapy, the cancer metastasized to his liver and his lung which resulted in numerous additional surgeries, and radiation. In the prior 18 months, while battling cancer, Deacon Hester's mother passed away. During the same period, he also lost a brother and a sister. The season was full of complex health challenges and loss, but Deacon Hester realized the difference in his disposition and fortitude was his strong relationship with Jesus Christ. He and his wife, Carrie never doubted that things would be ok. And at the time of the interview, they were still standing firm on their faith.

During this period of tremendous trials, Deacon Hester had served as the Chairman of the Deacon/Deaconess Ministry at Antioch Baptist Church for 23 years and recognized the fact that church members, family and friends would wonder, 'can he walk the walk?' He knew folks had watched his servant leadership and commitment to being there for others, but sensed they were watching how he handled his own season in the valley. Deacon Hester credited God for allowing him to withstand the challenges. He was blessed to continue to walk the walk, and he prayed that his manner had been a source of encouragement to others when they found themselves in the midst of such trials. His mantra was: "Keep your trust and faith in God."

Deacon Hester found that helping others, redirecting attention from himself and concentrating on others was therapeutic for him. He knew that once we commit to a relationship with Christ, He will make it known what He desires for you to do. It then only becomes a matter of making yourself available. And he reminded that no matter what you're going through, giving of yourself and serving others is therapeutic. We members and leaders in Antioch Baptist Church watched through every phase of his own battles and challenges, but Deacon Hester remained focused on how he could help and uplift others, whether spiritually, materially, professionally or otherwise. This demonstrated the essence of his servant leadership.

Psalms 34:9, was a comfort to Deacon Hester. It states: *Many are the afflictions of the righteous, but the Lord delivered him from them all.* Deacon Hester recognized in this scripture that he nor anyone else is exempt from life's challenges, but believers in the Lord have the assurance of His deliverance from these challenges. Waiting patiently, as the Bible says, when you are going through life situations is not easy. Deacon Hester stated, "It is easier to suggest to someone to wait patiently on the Lord than it is to do it. In those midnight hours, in those times when you're hospitalized there by yourself, when things look dire, waiting patiently is really tough. But the Word tells us to do that. That is a directive, and when we do it, looking back, we see that the hand of God is working."

Before we ended our conversation, Deacon Hester shared what the Holy Spirit was nudging him to do next. He explained it this way, "Well God has placed on my heart the desire to establish what we're calling a cancer exchange ministry within our church. We currently have a breast cancer awareness ministry but as we are all aware there are a number of cancers and other diseases affecting people. So, God pressed on my heart and I sought and got the pastor's approval to establish a Cancer Exchange Ministry which will be a two-way dialogue to exchange cancer related information as a way of encouraging patients, caregivers, family and friends. We look forward to kicking this off in February 2016. And again, I think it will be a blessing to the members, not only those with cancer but other life situations."

Deacon Lawrence 'Larry' Hester set a tremendous standard of dedication and commitment to serving God's people. God called him home to eternal rest in September 2016. For the way you glorified God, your superb care and love of God's people, your leadership, your faith and vision, you will never be forgotten and we owe you our deepest gratitude!! Servant Leader, Deacon Larry Hester, Rest in Heaven.

REFLECTIONS FOR YOU:

1. As you read Deacon Hester's story, what came to mind about your own journey?

2. Have you ever gone through multiple major challenges in the same time period? How did you keep going?

3. Have you experienced a season of having to "wait patiently"? What did you learn during the wait?

BE THE CHANGE YOU WANT TO SEE: PART II - JAMEECE PINCKNEY

In the same way, let your light shine before others, so that they may see your good works and give glory to your Father who is in heaven. (Matthew 5:16)

Jameece Pinckney is a senior executive with nearly twenty years of experience in the government contracting industry. Her past leadership roles include contract management, finance and accounting, procurement, risk management and business ethics. She holds a master's certificate in government contracting from George Washington University, a Juris Doctor from the University of Cincinnati College of Law, a Certification in Medical Technology from Meharry Medical College, and she holds both Master's and Bachelor's degrees from Tennessee State University. Jameece is the founder and chairman of the OPHELIA Foundation, a grassroots nonprofit 501c (3) she established in 2014 based upon the principle of helping others. The foundation's goal is to create opportunities to provide hope, empower lives and influence advancement. Jameece has been an active member of Delta Sigma Theta Sorority Inc, and she had served on the Northern Virginia Alumnae Chapter (NoVAC) Executive Committee for the past six years during our conversation.

When you read this biographical sketch, what words come to mind? Do you think of descriptions like accomplished, successful leader, caring, influential, visionary? It would make sense. She sounds like a woman driven to be a leader and someone who makes a positive difference in the lives of others. But people tend to view others through the present-day lens of their successes. Jameece says herself that people tend to look at "what appears to be your glory, without knowing your story." She likes the idea of people being able to see and understand some of her back story, that she did not magically arrive at where she is today. In fact, a look back shows where God has brought Jameece from.

Jameece grew up in Gary, Indiana when it had become a more impoverished city, and a majority African American city. Jameece grew up with a single mom, and as the oldest of five girls. She became the 'psuedo-caregiver' for her sisters as she watched her mom work really, really hard to make ends meet for their family. During a part of her growing up years, Jameece had a stepfather also in the home, but a time came when the family had to escape her stepfather's violent behavior.

In school, Jameece found a safe haven from some of the turbulence in her home environment. She fell in love with music as early as second grade. She did so well academically that she received a double promotion in school, but her Mom did not concur, and chose for her to stay with her class. Jameece continued to flourish with music under the band director, Mr. Ray Phillips from sixth grade on. Jameece, a gifted saxophone player, was one of the few female sax players in the area at the time. Music was quite an outlet for her, and she considered herself the best sax player. While the Gary environs were impoverished, Jameece and her family did not focus on that. Rather, they focused on what was in front of them, or more simply, they made the best of what they had.

Her Mom and her four younger siblings relocated from Gary to Atlanta the year before Jameece finished high school. Jameece remained in Gary and lived with her best friend and family to finish high school there. She relied on her guidance counselor, Dorothy Means, and her biology teacher, Jacqueline Ross, for support and help with personal needs, along with the help of other angels, particularly her best friend Keith Bryant's mom. When her mom left for Atlanta, Jameece had only $100 to care for her sisters and pay her school fees. She lost her wallet with the $100 in it, and it was Ms. Bryant who replaced the $100 and told Jameece to just pay it forward. Without them, Jameece acknowledged, she could not have accomplished the things she accomplished. Her class at Roosevelt High was very competitive academically. With her strong commitment to her studies, Jameece finished high school, 20th in her class of nearly 500. Wow!

Having grown up in a faith-filled home, it was no surprise that Jameece mentioned faith as her first core value, along with hard work to be able to sustain success, patience in order to persevere through challenges, and having the ability to walk in love - but never being run over. She also valued being fierce in all that you do, determination, focus and finally integrity, because you are only as good as your name and your word.

How did Jameece come to head a nonprofit foundation? The answer is reflected in enduring her tough early years and her desire to help and uplift others. The spirit of helping others and wanting to give back took root in action after Jameece finished law school and returned home to Gary. Jameece and one of her best friends, Barry Satterfield started a scholarship named in honor of Keith Bryant, one of their friends who passed away. They awarded the scholarship to an eighth grader and a 12th grader each year. Once Jameece moved to the D. C. area, the scholarship continued through the hands of her former band director, Ray Phillips who was then serving as band director for the eighth grade. When he transitioned to the high school, they continued the scholarship for a few more years. The next juncture was as Jameece's 40th birthday came into view. A party was planned, and Jameece was inspired to ask that instead of gifts for her, that her guests would donate 40 dollars to help 40 kids go back to school in the fall. That was the beginning of getting backpacks for kids in the community. Jameece worked with her friends who were teachers and educators in the local school systems beginning in 2011. By 2014, the desire expanded because people were pouring into that ministry to help the school kids, and the OPHELIA Foundation was established. The mission of the OPHELIA Foundation is to enable **O**pportunities to **P**rovide **H**ope, to **E**mpower lives and **I**nfluence **A**dvancement. The first letter of each letter of their mission spells OPHELIA. It is based on the principle of helping others. The name OPHELIA actually means *help* in Greek!

The name, OPHELIA was perfect not only for the planned helping mission. But OPHELIA was the name the Lord gave to Jameece as a legacy to her grandmother Ophelia! And furthermore, her husband's mother was also named Ophelia! The name of the OPHELIA Foundation honors them and symbolizes all women who helped their families. Jameece recognized that our mothers and our grandmothers are where we go for comfort. Who do we turn to or count on if no one else treats us kindly? It's almost universal that we can go to our mamas and grandmas.

Jameece serves as the Founder and Chairman, and her husband Gil serves as Vice Chairman. And the support continues from friends who really bought into the vision and mission of the foundation. At the time of this interview, the OPHELIA Foundation had just held their third annual fundraising event. The ongoing core focus areas for the foundation spell PHEAST – poverty, health, education, arts, sports and technology.

Through a revelation Jameece had, she knew that the OPHELIA Foundation was something she was supposed to do. God spoke to Jameece to think about her names and who she was. He led her to her high school memory book, where she had recorded lots of memories but had not looked at the book in years. Help and helping others was the theme of this organization she had created. She felt led to look at the several different last names she'd had since she was born. Jameece's last name at birth was the family name, Hill. Later, Jameece's name was changed to her birth father's last name, Eskridge. When her Mom later married, she was adopted by her stepfather and she became Jameece Latimer at adoption. Not listed in her high school memory book but when she got married, her last name became Pinckney. **H**ill, **Es**kridge, **L**atimer and **P**inckney. What other than a divine revelation led Jameece to discover that the first letter of each of the last names she had carried spelled the word HELP! Wow!

Although Jameece openly conveyed that her early years were not easy, her faith kept showing up just as she showed up, believing and trusting what God could do. She described a few pivotal moments where uncertainty reigned, but she relied totally on her faith.

One period was when she finished high school and it was time to go off to college. Her mom hired someone to take her from Atlanta to Tennessee State University. She was dropped off to get ready for band camp before all the other students arrived. The only certainty Jameece had upon arrival at school was that she had five scholarships in one pocket, and she had a bag with a set of new sheets and one outfit in her hand, and that was it. In the midst of all the longings, all the change and uncertainty being on her own in a new environment, she remembered it was just her and God. And Jameece excelled in college!!

Another huge step of faith during a time of uncertainty and challenge was after she finished law school and went back home. She found solace back at her home church where she spent time praying and seeking direction from God on what would be the next step in her career. She knew she had to, and would get beyond that particular moment. This was yet another critical juncture in Jameece's life, like her earlier challenge of heading off to college alone. Such moments seemed to yield the most inspiration and courage for her. She kept asking the Lord, "Where am I going? What is my direction? What do I do?"

After all the signs and research seemed to point to the East Coast, Jameece soon felt led to buy a one-way airline ticket from Chicago to Washington, DC. Her friend gave her a large military duffel bag, and she filled it with everything that she could. Whatever didn't make it into the bag, didn't go with her. The young man who drove her to the airport just couldn't believe it as they conversed, that she was going to a new place and was not sure what she was going to do when she got there. She explained that when the plane landed, God would guide her to where she was supposed to go. On October 14, 2004, she left everything behind, trusting the Lord to make a difference and to show her the direction to take. And Jameece has never looked back. From day one, she built a new life for herself in Washington, DC. She is a walking testament to living a faith that if you believe you can achieve something, you can see it and you can do it! This has been Jameece's mantra.

By the way…The young man who drove her to the airport in Chicago when she headed to Washington, DC with a one-way ticket, is now an ordained minister. Jameece was able to travel back to Chicago to attend his ordination service. At that time, Pastor Keith shared with her that he never had a firsthand observation of faith as strong as what she displayed with him on that drive to the airport back 15 years earlier. He shared what a revelation and inspiration that she was for him that day!

Jameece's tough, gritty early years may have been enough to cause irrevocable harm to someone else. But instead, through her challenges, Jameece had the faith, resilience and determination to succeed, which was incredibly transformational! With her strong desire to excel, and the creation of a foundation dedicated to helping others grow and achieve their dreams, Jameece has shown us the power of faith and we all bear witness to her living out the quote often attributed to Mohandas Ghandi, "Be the change you want to see in the world." While that was synonymous with Ghandi's philosophy, what he actually stated was, "If we could change ourselves, the tendencies in the world would also change. As a man changes his own nature, so does the attitude of the world change towards him." Jameece did not sit in her circumstances expecting change. She knew the changes she desired for her life and she set forth a model of faith and bold actions to achieve the changes she desired in her life. How prophetic, courageous and inspiring!!

Since our interview, Jameece has continued to be a fierce leader and a highly influential helper. She has served as President of the Northern Virginia Alumnae Chapter of Delta Sigma Theta Sorority from 2018-2020 and is the proud recipient of the 1st NoVAC Nellie Brooks Quander Distinguished Service Award! She is a graduate of the Small Business Administration (SBA) Emerging Leaders Class of 2019 CEOs, has been selected to serve as a Bizwomen Mentor by the Washington Business Journal (WBJ) for four consecutive years since 2018 and has been cited by the WBJ on mentoring during the Covid-19 pandemic. Jameece is one of four winners of the Vera Bradley Women of Inspiration Awards which will garner national attention for the OPHELIA Foundation. Jameece shared that all of the recognition is nothing but the uncommon favor of the Lord!

The OPHELIA Foundation is thriving with more

partnerships and giving more hope and support to more children. Jameece has also hung her own shingle as Founder, President and CEO of HyQuest Consulting Solutions, LLC. HyQuest, a minority and economically disadvantaged woman-owned small business, provides mission support services to its federal and commercial clients.

Jameece reflects in amazement that our careers are what we are paid for, but not everyone recognizes that your calling is what you are made for. While she is walking in hers, she sees that not everyone actually lives life walking in their calling. For Jameece D. Pinckney, she continues to demonstrate the strength and boldness of her faith, as she walks in her calling, and her purpose. Jameece continues to be the change she wants to see in the world!!

REFLECTIONS FOR YOU:

1. What did you remember about your own life as you read Jameece's story?

2. How did the boldness of Jameece's faith affect you?

3. What is one 'change' that you want to be?'

4. What will be your first step?

FULFILLMENT AWAITS – REV. COZY BAILEY

As each has received a gift, use it to serve one another, as good stewards of God's varied grace: whoever speaks, as one who speaks oracles of God; whoever serves, as one who serves by the strength that God supplies—in order that in everything God may be glorified through Jesus Christ. To him belong glory and dominion forever and ever. Amen. (Peter 4:10-11)

When is the last time you had a conversation with someone where you both got beneath the surface expressions of 'everything is fine' or 'I'm doing well?' Sometimes in deeper conversations, we hear the mention of a desire for something more or different in their lives. And often, when people express what they want more of, it falls under the umbrella of wanting more fulfillment.

There may be several reasons why people have not pursued more fulfillment in their lives. They may not know how. In conversation, it's common to hear responses that sounds like they missed the boat, such as: "I should have," "I wish I had" or "If only I had." And unfortunately, they may not have a clear idea about what they can do right now, in their current season, to find the fulfillment they long for. Some of you reading this may even be experiencing something similar.

The good news is that it's never too late to pursue fulfillment in our lives. And pursuing fulfillment may be simpler than you think. For believers in Christ, it is usually tied to learning your strengths and spiritual gifts, and then using them to make a positive difference in the lives of others. Why are these key factors? Your strengths and spiritual gifts are a part of your unique design by the Creator. By knowing these characteristics, an individual will then be able to leverage their uniqueness (strengths and spiritual gifts) to have more impact. In other words, in any situation, you know what you bring to the table. When you learn your strengths and gifts and allow their expression, you go beyond yourself and begin to contribute to a greater good and impact in the world, even if it is one person at a time.

Cozy Bailey's story can shed some insight on how fulfillment comes from knowing and using your strengths and spiritual gifts to uplift others. First, here's a little of his background. Cozy grew up in the inner city of St Louis, Missouri, being the eldest of seven children. While his parents had very modest means, they were not poverty stricken. There was always food on the table. At the age of eight, an event occurred that unbeknownst to Cozy at the time, would be a game changer for his future.

In the second grade, Cozy's teachers noticed that he had an advanced ability to read and told his parents he might be a candidate for the school's gifted and talented program. Cozy completed a series of tests and advanced from second grade to fourth grade! Through the gifted and talented program, Cozy received a superior education which helped to open bigger doors for him a little later. And what a benchmark Cozy set for his younger siblings as three others followed him and were also advanced from the second to the fourth grade due to their abilities!

As Cozy approached high school graduation, he had a dilemma because he had taken so many advanced academic courses that his school counselors and teachers affirmed that he was a natural to move on to a college education, even though that was not necessarily the norm for his neighborhood or relatives. Cozy's dilemma was that he had no money for college. He knew it would take all scholarship and possibly getting a job for him to go to college. Cozy performed really well on the standardized tests and actually began getting some good scholarship offers. He visualized being able to go to college and pursue a career in a technical field. He planned to pursue his interest in engineering even though he still knew that getting through college would be tough because of financial issues.

About that time, a fellow member of the high school track team shared that he was going to the Naval Academy. Cozy had no legacy of military in his family and was not familiar with the different branches of service. His friend gave him a book that explained everything about the Naval Academy. Cozy particularly noted that the Naval Academy paid your college costs; midshipmen received a salary, and graduates had a job guarantee for five years after graduation. For Cozy, the Naval Academy sounded like a winner! Cozy became a patriot through his experience at the Naval Academy and subsequently as an officer in the United States Marine Corps. Was it serving his country that began Cozy on a path of true fulfillment in his life? Is this when he learned his strengths and spiritual gifts? Let's see what unfolded for him.

During this season of his life, Cozy was still at an early

stage of growing and learning more about himself and more about God. Things were moving along smoothly for him, a young Marine Corps officer, his wife and their son. However, five years into his marriage, a season of challenge arose for him and his family. At 27 years of age, Cozy received orders for an unaccompanied tour to Okinawa Japan - which meant his wife and son could not go with him. The family would be separated.

With his family in St Louis Missouri and him in Okinawa, Japan, Cozy found himself experiencing depression. The depression led him to making extremely bad decisions in his professional life. He became very full of himself and nobody could tell him anything. His world of being the smartest guy around came crashing down upon him after an unfortunate conversation he had with an officer who outranked him. Cozy suffered the consequences of his actions. This incident knocked him down a couple of notches. And to make matters worse, towards the end of his 10-month Japan assignment, Cozy received notification that his wife had been in a car accident where she was seriously injured. There he was halfway around the world in Okinawa. How did the Baileys get through this?

Up until now, Cozy's story showed what can happen to any of us during a difficult season. We can spiral down with poor decision-making, or we may even dwell on "why is this happening to me?" But when we persevere and cope, it really prepares us for the next season and gives us hearts of gratitude for how we walked in faith. We can look back and see that the challenging times didn't overcome us; we can see the role that faith played in getting us through those challenges.

Thankfully, Cozy's wife, Andrea made a full recovery from her accident and he returned home from Okinawa. It was at this time that Cozy and Andrea began to grow not gradually, but exponentially in their spirituality. It was through prayer, reflection, perseverance and determination that they made it through. While they still faced rough spots, it was during this period that they joined hand in hand and began a stronger spiritual journey that continues to this day after 40+ years of marriage. The Baileys became active in their church for the first time in their marriage and assumed leadership roles, continuing to move forward. Cozy recalls their pastor at the time saying he saw greater service for both of them. Today Cozy believes the pastor saw then what he and Andrea are doing today. Through what they saw at one of their lowest points, Cozy and Andrea have grown to spiritual heights they never imagined.

It sounds like the Baileys began finding fulfillment!! How did Cozy's strengths and gifts come into the equation? During our interview, Cozy identified his strengths as being a gifted leader, an organizer, and he knew how to see and fix problems. His shared his spiritual gifts as exhortation, preaching God's word to God's people, and discernment. He has found that he has used both his strengths and his spiritual gifts especially now in his later years, in order to fulfill the roadmap that God has for him. He learned to lean upon his faith, which caused him to quit trying to exercise his worldly knowledge that people were so impressed with and to literally instead, let go and let God speak through him and through the spiritual gifts God had given to him.

Clearly over the years, Cozy has demonstrated 'letting go and letting God' in his life. After a 22-year successful military career, he retired and joined a prominent Information Technology services company, EDS, where he was the key person responsible for signing the largest IT outsourcing contract at that time in the history of the IT business, of $6.9B!! Along the way, he found time to attend seminary at Virginia Union University and became an associate minister, Sunday school teacher and active participant in the spiritual cancer support and member care ministries at First Mount Zion Baptist Church in Dumfries VA. How fulfilling it must be to use your strengths and gifts to make such a difference in the lives of others!

Cozy depicted one last powerful example of finding fulfillment by using his strengths and gifts to uplift others. At the time of our interview, he spoke passionately about his work, as the President of the Prince William County branch of the NAACP. Prince William County has experienced quite an explosion of population growth and diversity. The NAACP branch's profile has risen significantly in the last ten years, as they have dealt with a variety of social justice and equality issues for not only African Americans, but for all people who need assistance, to include special outreach to the area's Latino and Muslim friends.

Cozy equated their NAACP work to what the Bible showed Jesus came to do: to free the oppressed. He helped those no one else would help. Cozy sees the work as a golden opportunity for him to emulate and try to live up to the precepts of Jesus. They successfully help people who have issues with the law, unfair treatment with businesses, school board decisions, and a variety of other concerns. Cozy calls the work he and his team perform, a labor of love and a constant labor, as not a day goes by when someone does not send an email or call when they do not know where else to go for help. God has inspired the NAACP team to reach across the chasm of unfamiliarity, recognizing those things that are similar and to be a part of the effort that pulls people together no matter what their background may be, in order for them to enjoy what God has for them.

Cozy Bailey beautifully exemplified and reminded us of the blessings of using your spiritual gifts and strengths in service to others! When you identify your strengths and spiritual gifts, you can begin to make a difference in your family, community, your region, nation and ultimately the world! We all have the opportunity to uncover our own strengths and gifts and then journey along with God as He provides opportunities for us to represent Him to the world. That's walking and living in fulfillment!!

REFLECTIONS FOR YOU:

1. What are your strengths? If you have not discovered them, ask yourself, what comes easy for you that may seem difficult for others to do? What do others compliment you on doing well? Ask someone who knows you well, what are you good at? The answers are most likely some of your strengths.

2. What are your spiritual gifts? If you don't know, you can find no-cost spiritual gifts surveys and more information online.

3. How could learning your spiritual gifts and strengths enrich this season of your life?

WHAT STORY DO YOU WANT YOUR LIFE TO TELL? – MICHAEL MARX

"Do not store up for yourselves treasures on earth, where moths and vermin destroy, and where thieves break in and steal. But store up for yourselves treasures in heaven, where moths and vermin do not destroy, and where thieves do not break in and steal. For where your treasure is, there your heart will be also. (Matt 6:19-21)

'What story do you want your life to tell?' is an incredibly valuable question to be asked or to ask ourselves from time to time. Our answer can help us focus on the things that matter most. And at the same time, it can help us shed or release the things that do not serve the story we want our lives to tell.

When I asked Michael Marx this question during an interview, he had already given this some thought and gave a poignant answer. Michael explained that when he's the guy in his elder years sitting on his porch with a basket next to him and he's reflecting back over his life, he wants to have no regrets in his basket. No regrets of wishing he had spent more time with his family. Michael wants it to be said that he spent a lot of time helping people. He made that his priority. In the end, he'd like to know that his time on this earth was spent in such a way that it wasn't about him. What clarity of purpose and desire Michael had! So how had he lived out his story up to this point? Let's take a look inside Michael's life and see.

Michael grew up in upstate New Jersey, just outside Manhattan, in a very tight knit community. Both of Michael's parents immigrated from Europe and came with a lot of harsh experiences from Germany during the war and directly after the war. America was like a new life, a new place and new beginning for them.

Like most kids in the 60s, Michael spent a lot of time watching television, but his fondest memories were of him being outside with his buddies building tree houses, playing in the pond, falling in the pond - just the freedom he had, and all of the kids in the neighborhood being together. A vital lesson that Michael learned from his parents while growing up that he still holds dear today is that life is all about moving forward. Even though his parents had experienced a lot of trauma in their lives uprooting themselves and coming to the United States, they did not let that deter or hold them down. His father always said what had happened was not important, it was the present and the future that mattered.

Michael adopted a core value of paying careful attention to how he spends his time, believing that it says even more about you than how you spend your money. How you spend your time is a reflection on what you do and who you are. For Michael, his most important use of time is helping people. His greatest fun, greatest joy and most meaningful thing he does with his time is helping others. Whether it's in a professional capacity that returns to him in financial gain or sometimes without a financial gain, what matters most to Michael at the end of the day is when he can say he used most of the day helping people.

Having enjoyed an incredibly diverse work-life, at the time of our conversation in 2017, Michael was serving as the President of the Christian Coaches Network International. He loved to get calls from members asking for help when they were ready to move forward on an issue or project. He enjoyed connecting, hearing their fascinating stories and figuring out ways to help them.

Michael spent years working abroad as well. For 23 years, he and his wife, Joy, lived and worked in Berlin and Hanover, Germany. Michael set up a consulting business, which allowed him to enjoy his passion for teaching as well. His wife set up a travel agency business for people in Germany who wanted to ski in the U.S. Rocky Mountains. During those years in Germany, some referred to Michael and his wife's roles as "tent making" missionaries. While they had paying jobs in Germany, Michael recognized they did a lot to serve the Lord. As we spoke, many years later back in the U.S., Michael still had clients in Germany.

When Michael and his wife returned to the United States, they chose not to decide immediately where they would live permanently. They bought and lived in an RV, traveling and working online for a year and a half. After that, they still did not immediately settle down. The following year and a half, they lived in the camper with it parked in Alaska which included two winters of minus 30-degree temperatures in order to fulfill one of his wife's dreams… to learn the ins and outs of professional dog-sledding and to establish her own dog-sledding business. Eventually they traded their RV for a dog truck, two sleds and a dozen sled-dogs, as they set up a home in Colorado at 8,100 feet, where today his wife is indeed running tours, Michael himself is running his coaching business, New Trails Coaching online and on Saturdays he's a ski instructor.

Who are the people who seek Michael's coaching? His clients are not looking to be pioneers, nor are they looking to be rich, or even first. They are people in mid-life transitions, who look forward to some exploration after having the first half of their lives spent chasing other people's dreams. They seek coaching as they want the next phase of their lives to uncover and chase their own dreams, and whatever God wants them to do. Michael's greatest joy is seeing them move from having a stalled life to a dynamic one.

Along Michael's diverse path, were there times when he was thrown a major curve ball or faced a major challenge? Absolutely. In fact, Michael noted that we all have examples where God has been really faithful to bring us through tough times. It's not a matter of if, but when a major challenge happens to each of us. And the example of a major challenge that Michael discussed was unrelated to the experiences he had shared up to that point.

In 2000, Michael was teaching a college course and enjoyed it very much because the college pretty much gave instructors free rein to manage the classes any way they wanted, as long as there was a rich curriculum and a final exam at the end of the course. The students really enjoyed Michael's class. To get his students thinking in preparation for their long essay final exam, he gave an example of the type of question they could receive for the exam. For giving the students the example question for the final exam, he was fired. Michael thought he was making a good pedagogical move, but the college administrators saw it differently. From their perspective, final exams were certified and the essay question was not allowed to be given to the students in advance. Although all he did was give an example, it was enough to cross the line and caused him to be fired. Michael was really, really hurt. But it opened his eyes to the fact that just because you are innovative and only intend to help people with pure intentions, you still might have a system around you that requires a certain type of checks and balances.

How did Michael's faith help him during this significant challenge? Michael had people praying for him, and while he felt vulnerable during that period, he felt God's assurance that he would get through the challenge. He sensed God telling him this was something he needed that would benefit others as he moved forward. Michael also strongly felt God's love, acceptance and forgiveness.

We can all relate to having good intentions or trying to do something good that gets misinterpreted or wrongly judged. When in such a situation, we may feel alone, or a lot of "why is this happening to me?". Sometimes as in Michael's case, God allowed his challenge to be purposeful and beneficial, just as Michael sensed during the difficulty that it would be.

How did Michael's challenging experience come to benefit others? As stated earlier, Michael had always felt called to help people. And eventually it was Christian coaches in particular that he helped to grow, and to look at where the guardrails were. Michael had come to understand that certain guardrails exist for a reason. Ultimately God positioned Michael to become a subject matter expert on ethics in Christian coaching!!

Michael was even approached by a publisher who recognized the need for a book on ethics for Christian coaches. When Michael saw how little written material there was in the marketplace, he agreed to write his book *Ethics and Risk Management for Christian Coaches*. His book distills what it means in practice to behave ethically. It highlights the positives versus the punitive aspects of ethical decision making. Michael also leads a Community of Practice on Ethics for the International Coach Federation (ICF) which emphasizes that ethics is a premise that really comes down to respect, and the ways to allow your respect for clients and others prevent your crossing the line into something unethical.

When Michael went through his challenge of being fired from teaching a course that he enjoyed, ethics as a subject was not on his radar. Yet he sensed that the experience he went through would be beneficial to others. And clearly God used the experience to give him a unique appreciation of ethics and the value of checks and balances. And indeed, God gave Michael a message to share that would be helpful to others.

So…as we scanned just some of the facets of Michael's life, we saw him being selfless and delighting in opportunities to help others. Michael's life illustrates his passion in putting the needs of others first. Surely, when Michael Marx is in his elder years, the story that his life will tell is, "He used his time to help others." And his regret basket will indeed be empty!

REFLECTIONS FOR YOU:

1. What did you recognize as a recurring thread through-out Michael's story?

2. What story do you want your life to tell?

3. Have you ever had good intentions but your acts were misinterpreted? How did you cope with the situation?

4. What is in your regret basket right now? What do you want to do about it?

WISDOM OF A 93-YEAR OLD

FAITH MANIFESTED OVER A LIFETIME –
MRS. PENNIA 'PENNY BELL' FORD

That your faith should not stand in the wisdom of men, but in the power of God. (1 Corinthians 2:5)

Faith. Love. Strength. Smarts. Joy. Fortitude. Generosity. Unflappable.

These words come quickly to mind to describe a woman whose story serves as an expression of love, and a bonus offering in this book of true-life stories. She is the embodiment of overcoming any and every life challenge through her faith in God. After this compilation project was near completion, there came an opportunity to interview this amazing woman, the one and only Mrs. Pennia Ford, warmly referred to as "Mrs. Penny Bell." As you will see, she lives the life of an overcomer who triumphs through faith.

In July 2020, Mrs. Penny Bell had to cope with the unthinkable. Her beloved son, Edwin Russell contracted Covid-19 and his condition worsened so quickly that within a very short time period, he passed away. What would a loss of this magnitude do to Mrs. Penny Bell? Those close to her, (including my husband and me) witnessed firsthand her unwavering faith and continued trust in the Lord even amidst the shock and grief of losing her son. Her faith ministered to us and others who struggled to accept the sudden death of her dear son. Not long after her son's death, Mrs. Penny Bell was moved from her long-term home in

Michigan, near her son, to Virginia. In November of 2020, she too was stricken with the Covid-19 virus. She was hospitalized and had to have weeks of rehabilitation. But thankfully for all who know and love her, she managed to resume her health after Covid-19. Today at 93 years of age, she declares, "God is not through using me yet!"

In a wide-ranging interview, Mrs. Penny Bell shared some of her life story and unadorned nuggets of wisdom. Selected parts of her story are chronicled here as a surplus or overflow to this compilation project; a handy reference to encourage and sow seeds of faith into readers. First is some of her background and perspectives.

Mrs. Penny Bell was born in 1928 and grew up in Kinston, North Carolina. President Hoover was in the White House and the country was in the throes of the Great Depression in her early years. During the Depression, she recalls hearing how even the rich and affluent people suffered. Even people with loads of money in banks lost everything.

Mrs. Penny Bell grew up in the close-knit Fields Family with her father Simon, a brick mason, her mother Hattie, a homemaker, her two brothers Simon Jr and Leon, and herself. When Mrs. Penny Bell was only seven years old, her five-year old baby sister Darnell died. She described this as a first experience with true heartache for her. After this point, the family doted on her all the more for fear of losing another child. She and her brothers were close, and whatever her brothers did, she did. Whether playing marbles or even climbing onto the roof of the house, she kept up with them. Some of her fondest early memories were times with her beloved grandma, who lived across the street. They made candy together and she enjoyed watching her grandma's ingenuity while sewing, knitting, making crafts and embroidering.

Considering this was the era of The Great Depression, Mrs. Penny Bell and her family fared pretty well. Her immediate family, extended family, neighbors and others pulled together and supported each other's survival. Her father's masonry trade and his work in the tobacco factories allowed him to make more than many common laborers in the Kinston area. In her family, they were never allowed to view themselves as well off, because that was a perspective that divided people. Her family were people of humility, who cared about the welfare of others.

That humility and a few other core values were instilled in Mrs. Penny Bell from an early age. She has held onto and lived these values throughout her life. She described them as:

- <u>Respect everyone, just as you do your own parents.</u> You are no better than anyone else and no one else is better than you. (Her mother worded it to her and her siblings this way): "If you're going down the street and see Mr. Jones, it's none of your business what Mr. Jones is doing - you run by him and yell back to say, Good Morning Mr. Jones, even if he's laying out there under the tree. Be respectful. And your business is to go and do what you were asked to do."

- <u>Faith is a part of living.</u> (There was never a time without faith in her life growing up or church all day on

Sunday. There wasn't any place else to go on Sundays but to church: from Sunday School, to worship service to a second Sunday School to Baptist Training Union in the evenings.

- <u>Prayer and the bible are intricate parts of life.</u> "Growing up, when you got up in the morning and after your mama cooked, you said your bible verse and grace before you ate. "Before I went to bed, I couldn't wait to kneel beside mama to say my prayers. By third grade I knew the 100th Psalm." While Mrs. Penny Bell didn't know it was faith, she knew that devotion and prayer brought order to her life. From her childhood up to the time her children were young with their grandmama, scriptures were taught and explained.

- <u>Helping others is important.</u> "When we saw others without, we believed in lending a hand." One case in point was when, after her Pastor, Rev Hodges' adult children moved to New York, they would send boxes of clothes by bus back to North Carolina. Mrs. Penny Bell would help a group of women fix those clothes and Rev Hodges would hang the items in his store. People who needed clothing could take what they needed and place whatever they could 'pay' in the big candy box as they left the store.

- Do not worry about what a person says, watch their actions. "People can say anything. But watch what they do. You will know who a person is by what they do."

- Nurture your marriage. "Value your partner and take time for and with one another. Live your love in the present. Carve out special times together, but also enjoy each other on a daily basis, at the end of the workday, even when it has to be for short periods of time. Do not wait for special occasions like birthdays, Valentine's Day, or holidays to express your love for your spouse: do it daily."

- Always apply yourself. This simple mantra was powerful enough that it passed down to influence Mrs. Penny Bell's four children to receive their post graduate educational degrees. And she herself later went back to school for advanced studies. Her willingness to apply herself allowed her to be trained to work in diverse career fields, from nursing to teaching to real estate and youth rehabilitation, as well as special education.

- Be very selective and careful with whom you choose to talk to about your struggles. "Only confide in someone you know is a friend indeed. Or choose a member of the clergy to speak with."

Mrs. Penny Bell reminisces today that her age group is the last of the "manual generation." That means what so many do today through automation and technology, her generation did it all manually. For example, there were no electric ovens, no microwave ovens, no slow cookers, no dishwasher, or washing machines. No internet, Google, smartphones, computers or iPads for quick access to any type of information you want. Wow, reflect for a moment on the conveniences of your life-styles today that you may often take for granted. None of those conveniences existed when Mrs. Penny Bell was growing up, or for much of her life. Yet her generation had the fortitude, faith and willingness to make their lives as full and meaningful as possible, given the harsh times they lived through.

When Mrs. Penny Bell finished Adkin High School, she enrolled at North Carolina College for Colored (NCCC), known today as North Carolina Central University (NCCU). She was not able to finish because during her first year, her mother became very ill. At that time, both of her brothers were in the military (Leon, in the Navy and Simon in the Air Force.) When her mama's condition did not get better, Mrs. Penny Bell did not return to NCCC, instead she stayed home to take care of her mama. This was when she truly realized the strength of her faith. She was frightened of her mama's weakened state, but she kept praying. Even in the middle of the night she'd kneel at her mother's bedside and talk with the Lord, seeking His guidance. Mrs. Penny Bell's mama was being treated by the one doctor who served black patients during that time period, Dr. Harrison, and who by that period of time had grown very old himself.

Mrs. Fields survived but was never as strong as she had been before. Eventually she had to have both of her legs amputated. Mrs. Penny Bell watched her mama just exist for a period of time. She even questioned the actions she had taken to help her mama. She became so consumed with her mama living that she did any and everything she could do for her. Once her mama got stronger and better able to manage, Mrs. Penny Bell got two relatives to stay with her each day while she drove from Kinston to Greenville, North Carolina for 18 months to complete a practical nursing course. After the course, the Lenoir Memorial Hospital hired her. While working at the hospital, Mrs. Penny Bell faced another one of her biggest heartaches. One morning while she was at work, Mrs. Penny Bell's beloved grandmother passed away. Her supervisor received the message that morning. However, it wasn't until the end of her workday that her supervisor, without any compassion or care, told her that her grandmother had passed that morning. Mrs. Penny Bell vividly recalls the anger and anguish she felt at not getting that news until the entire workday had passed. By the time she arrived home, her grandmother's remains, her bed and everything had been taken away. This seemed too much for her to bear at the time.

Eventually Mrs. Penny Bell decided it was time for her to leave Kinston. She took her Aunt Bertha up on her offer to fund her attending business school if she would move to Philadelphia. And that's what Mrs. Penny Bell did! She got involved in real estate and received her business license. Mrs. Penny Bell lived on Martin Street directly across the street from the renowned singer, Marian Anderson. In Philadelphia, she met and married her husband, Harold Russell. He was not happy with her doing real estate work, going to show houses with different men and women that they knew nothing about. So, Mrs. Penny Bell soon gave up her real estate career and she and her husband began their family of three children.

Before long, Mrs. Penny Bell had to face a major life transition. When she had two children under three and was pregnant with her third child, she and her husband got a divorce. From that point on, it was just her and her kids. Later, she explored and found career pursuits, some of which allowed her to grow academically right along with her children. As an example, she stated that when her kids studied new math, Mrs. Penny Bell and several of the other moms went back to school and also studied new math.

Once her children were old enough to stay home without her, she really pursued her own education and career with vigor! She learned about career opportunities for people who did academic community work. She and five other women availed themselves of every relevant educational opportunity that came their way. Mrs. Penny Bell studied at Temple University and the University of Pennsylvania.

To say that Mrs. Penny Bell did not choose a traditional learning and growth path would be an understatement! She sought firsthand life enriching experiences that others only read or heard about. She traveled to Israel with a 12-member team from Temple University where she had an opportunity to teach at the University of Tel Aviv, just as Israel was becoming more modernized. Through her travel and tours in Israel, the setting strengthened her faith. Seeing the Dead Sea Scrolls and where they were found, for example, made her home bible studies come alive.

Back in Philadelphia, ten years after her first marriage, Mrs. Penny Bell met and married her soulmate, William J. Ford. She recounts her husband as a marvelous man, husband and father. Mr. Ford not only became a doting father to Mrs. Penny Bell's three children, but they also had a daughter together, something Mr. Ford had always wanted. He was a wonderful father to all four children and lived to help them all and see them all through college before he died. Mrs. Penny Bell and her beloved husband had many rich years and memories together before his passing.

During the Clinton Administration, at which point her children were all adults and established in their careers, Mrs. Penny Bell had the opportunity to live and teach in West Africa. Her extended periods there added up to almost three years given her time in Gambia, Ghana, Malawi, Benin, and Cameroon. She accepted assignments through *Teachers For Africa*, created by Rev. Dr. Leon Sullivan, to help establish school systems and structures that would allow the countries to begin to function more independently. Not only did she experience the different cultures and see the potential in those countries, but she also saw the institutionalized racism and the self-hatred and inferiority that it created which kept people believing their potential was extremely limited.

Did Mrs. Penny Bell face other personal trials after the loss of her husband and during her years of work in Africa? She certainly did. One story illustrates how she lived out her faith when she was neck-deep in a difficult trial so far from home. While working in West Africa, Mrs. Penny Bell and her roommate went on a holiday to South Africa and decided to take a tour of a gold mine. The two of them along with five or six others, took a crude elevator shaft to go down into the mine to observe what took place firsthand. But the cables carrying the elevator shaft suddenly broke and the car fell at least four stories before it wedged into one side of the mountain. Mrs. Penny Bell hit her head sharply when the elevator crashed. Her roommate broke her wrist and there were injuries of other people inside as well due to the sudden impact. But there was nothing they could do, no telephone to call for help, and no ambulances nearby. They were stuck in a mineshaft until whenever help would arrive.

Nonetheless, inside that dark, damp mineshaft, wedged into one side of a mountain, due to the weight of the people piled on the floor on one side of the elevator, Mrs. Penny Bell knew to pray. The depth of her faith kept her from feeling despair or panic. She simply prayed hard that the elevator would not careen any further down the mineshaft. She remembers praying, "God you are my friend, and you will take care of me." She grabbed just one verse from the bible and meditated on it as they waited for help to arrive. On that day she chose Psalm 16:1 *Preserve me O God, for in thee do I put my trust.* Eventually, they were rescued from the mineshaft safely. They knew they walked away from a situation that could have ended a whole lot worse. Mrs. Penny Bell knew that God's grace had spared them.

Thankfully when they returned to their homestead in West Africa, the doctor did not find any serious injuries.

Along this believer's phenomenal journey, you've glimpsed that she has dealt with the kind of risk, heartaches, trials and obstacles that might have destroyed or flattened others. But not Mrs. Penny Bell. Whatever she's facing, just like she did in the mineshaft in South Africa, she says she'll grab one bible verse to meditate on. She has cultivated the practice of keeping her eyes looking toward her faith, believing "We've come this far by faith." And in the meantime…

What is Mrs. Penny Bell doing today? She lives in an assisted living facility in Virginia, with a mind, wit and spirit as sharp as ever! There she ministers to facility staff, care providers and other residents despite her physical limitations. At 93 years of age as mentioned earlier, she declares, "God is not through using me yet. Faith is what prompts me…what moves me forward. Every morning when I wake up, I say, thank you God. Even if my body is hurting, I say, what is it that you want me to do today? Who do you want me to be a light to today?"

Wow, Mrs. Pennia "Penny Bell" Ford is still generous, being a light, getting up in love; still showing Christ to others, still holding to God's Unchanging Hand and still being joyful; the same things she has always done. How inspiring to see such faith manifested over her entire lifetime!! Glory to God!! If Mrs. Penny Bell, in her 90th decade of living is still faith-filled, giving, serving and loving others, may you be inspired and convicted to do the same at whatever age or stage of life you are in today!! God is a Wonder!!

REFLECTIONS FOR YOU:

1. What did you personally discover as you read Mrs. Penny Bell's story?

2. What are you inspired to do differently in your life after reading her story?

3. Who comes to mind that you can be a "Mrs. Penny Bell" (encourager, faith-filled, inspiration) for?

4. Who has been a "Mrs. Penny Bell" in your life that you want to show your appreciation to?

MORE ON THE OVERCOMERS

1. Dale Fletcher's Bible study about spirit, mind and body health, PathWay 2 Wholeness, is now available for purchase as a self-paced program and can be found on his ministry website www.faithandhealthconnection.org. He continues to provide support to his wife, Janice's business and ministry, Christian Coach Institute, where she educates, equips and encourages Christian coaches around the world. Dale and Janice make a habit of enjoying homemade pizza on most Friday nights.

2. Brenda and Jeff Gaines are world travelers and love exploring different countries and their culture. Brenda owns a professional consulting company focused on hiring great people to achieve great things. Jeff started a podcast called Reverend G's Words of Encouragement at www.rg-woe.com where he provides short impactful sermons for life's journey.

3. Joanne Lattimore is working on her second book entitled "My 5 Girls: The Journey". The timeframe for its release is Spring 2022. Since turning age 70, she has

acquired a desire to speak. She believes there is someone whose life can be touched or even changed by hearing her story. She's become an active member of Les Brown's global, motivational speaking group called "Hungry To Speak" attending virtual weekly meetings with him and her son.

4. Michael E. Coppedge, now retired, has lived by God's grace a blessed life, in some seventeen different countries as a US federal servant, preacher, teacher, counselor and missionary. He's been married to his bride for 49 years, and their union has been blessed with one daughter, a son-in-law and two grandchildren.

5. Jameece Pinckney lives in Northern Virginia, where she and her husband Gil oversee her consulting firm (www.hyquestconsulting.com) and her charitable foundation (www.opheliafoundation.org). Jameece is also active in her church and as a member of Delta Sigma Theta Sorority, Inc.

6. Lonnie and Delores Williams just recently celebrated their 30th wedding anniversary. In this season, through some health challenges, they remain well in spirit and have begun to cherish and embrace a joy, through expressions of love heaped upon them by 11 grandchildren and two great-grandchildren. Pure unencumbered Joy! Lonnie and Delores also remain committed to experience quiet time each day with Jesus.

7. Joe Alexander is a retired Army Officer and a Director with Grant Thornton LLP. He and his wife live in Northern Virginia where he enjoys spending time with his granddaughter, playing golf, teaching Bible Studies at his church and substituting at local high and middle schools.

8. Alia Watkins is retired from Federal Service and is living her best life, enjoying time and traveling with family & friends. She and her husband of 23 years serve their community by taking on long-term substitute teaching positions. Alia also established ministries for at-risk children in her community through summer camps and after school programs with tutoring during the school year.

9. Dr. Marshal Ausberry, in addition to serving as Pastor of Antioch served as the 1st Vice President of the Southern Baptist Convention (SBC), (2019-2021), and served as President of the National African American Fellowship of the SBC (2018-2021).

10. Tony and Sue Stamilio recently celebrated their 47th anniversary and moved to a home they built in Central PA. They love to spend time with their two daughters and three grandchildren exploring PA and traveling the world to discover history and art. Tony is an avid fly fisherman and enjoys woodworking projects. He continues his coaching practice with a passion to support

leaders and their organizations in becoming the "best versions of themselves" (first-step-coaching.com).

11. Sister Rochella Marable is currently a member of Antioch Baptist Church, where she is Director of Women's Ministry, People Care Coordinator and Friday Morning Bible Study teacher. She loves spending time with her husband and children, and finding her fountain of youth in the hearts and minds of her adorable six grandkids, whom she calls her "Sugar Babies".

12. Felicea Meyer-DeLoatch is a practicing Licensed Clinical Social Worker in Fairfax, Virginia. She is looking forward to opening a nonprofit behavioral health clinic in the Northern Virginia area in the fall of 2023. She and her staff will train practitioners to work within diverse communities while turning no child, youth, or family away due to inability to pay for services. The website to the Growth and Healing HUB is www.gandh.org

13. Jim and Jean Jones continue to be blessed and well. Jean continues to work at Youth for Tomorrow, a group home for disadvantaged youth. Jim just turned 80 years old and is a great fisherman, who cleans the fish and gives them to his friends. They spend quality time caring for their youngest two of seven grandchildren, Cayson 4, and Kai, 18months. They greatly enjoy being Leaders of the Elderly Ministry at their church.

ACKNOWLEDGMENTS

A number of people have helped and influenced this book coming to fruition. Some of whom have poured their love, mentoring and support into me far before this season of my life. I'd like to thank:

My husband, Richard 'Spike' Jones. I'm so blessed by all of the ways you've supported me on this incredible book-writing journey. But I'm also grateful for all of the ways that you support me and love me every day. You are the best husband ever and I love you endlessly!!!

My parents Nimrod Stephens Sr and Annie Stephens, who gave me all that you knew to give; your best helped to mold my life and my faith. To my bonus Mom, Alma P. Stephens, who showed me by her example what was possible. I hope each of you are smiling about this project from above. I always carry your light with me. I love you and I miss you so much.

To my 'specials' and mentors who have poured love and wisdom into me, and have been such generous, powerful influences in my life that you helped to carry me to this season of book writing: My late Aunt Fannie Walker, cousins, the late Wana Grace Bishop, Henry & Burnice Patterson, my darling mother-in-love,

Mrs. Margaret Colson, Mrs. Ethel Pressley, Elizabeth 'Liz' Hurt, Charles & Peggy Brooks, Ray & Donna Mobley, Donna Ray, the late Honorable Ruby DeMesme, Deaconess Margaret Boone and Janice LaVore-Fletcher. What a difference you have made in my life and I love you all very much.

To three sisterfriends who believed in this book idea and encouraged its creation. Thank you for agreeing to be my first editors along with Spike, putting fresh eyes on my draft stories, Angelia Atkins, Denise Perryman and Joyce Harris. I cannot thank you enough!! This project would not be a 'book' today if you had not supported me like you did. You are extra special blessings in my life.

To three young people that I could not love more if they were my own children, my nephew, Rod (& Jessica) Stephens and nieces, Patrice Hall and Stephanie Stephens. I am so blessed by the countless ways you and your children enrich my life!! Ashley Brinkley, Victoria Melendez, Tyler Savage and Madisyn Howard, you all are on the list of my loves always. I'm sooo proud of each of you!

To Linda Griffin, my publishing coach, thank you for all of your expertise and support, walking me through your step-by-step process to get my draft manuscript across the finish line to become this book! Special thanks to Kiah Spinks, Esq and Kenya Savage for your assistance! And special thanks to Russ Terry at Life Coach Radio Network.

To every encourager in my life, whether you are family, sorors or friends, you know who you are. I so appreciate having you in my life for your thoughtfulness, joyful spirit and support not only with this project, but always.

Most importantly, to My Savior Jesus Christ, thank you for equipping me for your purposes and for the gift of salvation. May you be known and glorified through this work!!